Personal Transformation
and a New Creation

Personal Transformation and a New Creation

The Spiritual Revolution of Beatrice Bruteau

Edited by
ILIA DELIO, OSF

ORBIS BOOKS
Maryknoll, New York 10545

ORBIS BOOKS
Maryknoll, New York 10545

Fathers and Brothers
MARYKNOLL™
TOGETHER IN GOD'S MISSION OF MERCY

Founded in 1970, Orbis Books endeavors to publish works that enlighten the mind, nourish the spirit, and challenge the conscience. The publishing arm of the Maryknoll Fathers and Brothers, Orbis seeks to explore the global dimensions of the Christian faith and mission, to invite dialogue with diverse cultures and religious traditions, and to serve the cause of reconciliation and peace. The books published reflect the views of their authors and do not represent the official position of the Maryknoll Society. To learn more about Maryknoll and Orbis Books, please visit our website at www.maryknollsociety.org.

Manufactured in the United States of America.

Manuscript editing and typesetting by Joan Weber Laflamme.

Library of Congress Cataloging-in-Publication Data

Names: Bruteau, Beatrice, 1930– honouree. | Delio, Ilia, editor.
Title: Personal transformation and new creation : essays in honor of Beatrice Bruteau / edited by Ilia Delio, OSF.
Description: Maryknoll : Orbis Books, 2016. | Includes bibliographical references and index.
Identifiers: LCCN 2016001639 | ISBN 9781626982093 (pbk.)
Subjects: LCSH: Bruteau, Beatrice, 1930– | Religion. | Theology.
Classification: LCC BL73.B785 P47 2016 | DDC 230—dc23 LC record available at https://lccn.loc.gov/2016001639

I would like to thank Sister Lisa Drover, OSF, for her assistance and my graduate assistant at Villanova University, Carl Vennerstrom, for constructing the timeline of Beatrice Bruteau's works. I am also grateful for the support and friendship of my Orbis manager, Michael Leach, whose unflagging enthusiasm for all things new continues to spur me on. A special thanks to Villanova University who hired me in the midst of another book and numerous public lectures. I am grateful for the support of the University and the time given to complete this book.

Contents

Part III
Teacher, Mentor, Friend

Introduction

ILIA DELIO

We can't solve problems
by using the same level of consciousness
and same kind of thinking
we used when we created them.
—ALBERT EINSTEIN

In November 2014, Cynthia Bourgeault and I were having dinner, recalling the recent death of Beatrice Bruteau. As we reminisced on the life of Beatrice and the profound impact she had on us as women writing theology in a new age, we also lamented that so few people were acquainted with her thought. We agreed that this brilliant, shining light of the twentieth century deserves public recognition; as a result, this collection of essays was born.

I shall not say too much in this brief introduction, as Cynthia has provided an excellent biographical sketch of Beatrice, a charming little woman with a fierce philosophical mind and a profound theological depth. Like Pierre Teilhard de Chardin, who had a significant influence on her thought, Beatrice had penetrating eyes, as if she saw what tomorrow could be in today's light. She probed the human psyche like a surgeon operating on delicate tissue. Her insights were borne aloft on a deep mystical spirit nurtured by Catholic Christianity and Vedantic Hinduism. Her unique interspiritual consciousness led her to see from a different center with keen insight, both mystical and intuitive. She was a contemplative thinker. The medieval theologian Bonaventure once said that knowledge is a stage on the journey to God. This was true of Beatrice. We see in her writings that knowledge is not its own end but moves us to a deeper understanding of the divine mystery, enkindling within us an inner depth of love. Her theology is based on participation of the knowing subject in spiritual realities. This means not simply engaging in intellectual thought but also being open to the gifts of the Holy Spirit and deepening the spiritual life. Her life and work reveal a theologian living in the depths of the divine Spirit, searching the realms of the Absolute and the secrets of divine Reality. As she professed throughout her writings, one must be free from the constraints of the ego in order to plunge into the mystery of God. This was true of Beatrice; she lived in the freedom of love.

Bruteau's contemplative approach to theology is holistic. Theology is not what one studies; rather, it is what one *does*. The real task of theology belongs to the life of the Spirit and grace, whereby one enters into the freedom of love that makes one whole and wholly participant in the evolution of God. Any strictly theological truth, one that has its roots in God, is not content with its unique objective determination. Rather, such truth takes on a performative sense, one that is transforming for the subject. Knowledge through love leads us to truth when it liberates us to evolve to higher levels of consciousness and spontaneous being-in-love.

Bruteau's theology rests on the vision of Pierre Teilhard de Chardin. Whereas Teilhard saw the grand cosmic scheme of Christ in evolution, Bruteau developed an understanding of the human person in evolution. She explored consciousness as an evolutionary development, from self-separateness to self-participation, and from the partial self to the whole self and the self that is part of the whole. She proposed that humanity is seeking a new self-understanding, away from the self as a separate entity to the self as intimately intertwined with other humans and the entire cosmos. A new type of "holistic consciousness" is emerging, she claimed, as humanity takes part in the evolutionary process. This new integral consciousness includes a new awareness of interbeing and interrelationality. This type of consciousness was expressed by Jesus of Nazareth, who in his Holy Thursday revolution overturned the tables of domination and power and ushered in a new communal wholeness of shared life. Bruteau describes this new communion paradigm as a pattern of relationships that sees the world as an organic whole, each element in relation to the other and interdependent with the other. The values of cooperation, sympathy, compassion, forgiveness, and a desire for the other's well-being lie at the heart of the communion model of shared humanity. Although she was deeply committed to her Catholic heritage, her vision of cosmic reality is a synthesis of Western and Eastern religions. She believed that spiritual energies must be harnessed for the forward movement of evolution through a type of interspiritual convergence. God is rising up through this evolutionary process as the unitive center of participative life, in which the unconscious and resistant are increasingly transcended in the freedom and creativity of love.

The essays in this volume serve as an introduction to Bruteau's life and thought. Cynthia Bourgeault's opening essay addresses the question most people ask: Who was Beatrice Bruteau? Here we meet Beatrice Bruteau the philosopher, wife, and contemplative theologian who influenced those around her in uncanny ways. Bourgeault's essay sets the tone for exploring Bruteau's theological and philosophical thought. To appreciate the contribution of Beatrice Bruteau is to see her work within a wider scope of the *Neofeminine,* a term that connotes deep relationality, unitive love, and wisdom. Ursula King's essay provides the scaffold for this collection of essays by asking whether there can be a feminine mystical way for the twenty-first century. This is an important question for Bruteau, who brought together science, philosophy, and theology in a way that reflected a new level of Neofeminine consciousness. The key for Bruteau is consciousness, and Barbara Fiand's essay elucidates her work on consciousness transformation, reflecting her emphasis that "we are inescapably creators of [our] future in the most fundamental sense of determining the basic value patterns of perception that order all other expeirences and thereby compose our human world." Cynthia Bourgeault offers an intriguing essay on a new understanding of Trinity as the ground of Bruteau's communal paradigm. A trinitarian dynamic, marked by the law of three, is a core metaphysical principle, according to Bourgeault, that undergirds an intrinsically relational universe.

One of the key aspects of Bruteau's thought is the ecstatic nature of God, who is rising up in and through the evolution of consciousness. Kerrie Hide writes:

> She [Bruteau] opens a pathway through the confines of our egoic mind into the non-dual consciousness of our Essential Self, to evolve in consciousness and awaken "communion" consciousness. She invites us into the involution that empowers evolution, so we may live in the ground of the ecstasy of *Agape*, of God creating the world and the world realizing God.

Hide's essay explores Bruteau's ecstatic God in the flow of love and evolutionary spiritual development.

Bruteau's world of deep relationality and divine indwelling in evolution gives rise to a new understanding of the human person and human community. Ilia Delio maps human evolution as a transition from the individual to that of person, following Bruteau's insights on consciousness. Consciousness of ourselves from the outside, Bruteau writes, is only a first stage of self-reflective consciousness. On the higher level of the human person we are impelled to realize ourselves as "conscious of being conscious," a noetic coincidence with ourselves as conscious acts of life-communicating life. This is the contemplative life of spiritual freedom by which we act out of our interior selves and by which we enter into the interiority of our fellow beings.

Brie Stoner, a young mother and budding scholar, offers a vision of theological hope for the millennial generation by highlighting the vision of Teilhard de Chardin. Just as Teilhard had a profound impact on Bruteau, Stoner shows how he also can have a deep impact on the millennial generation. Teilhard felt that what the modern lacks is not religion but unsatisfied theism; our current lack of religious interest demonstrates the failure of religion to animate the human spirit. Similarly, Stoner sees Teilhard's vision as one birthing something new in our midst. Kathy Duffy offers new insight on Teilhard's *Mass of Creation* as a liturgical prayer that help can change our awareness as persons, that is, as deeply connected beings who are one with the whole cosmos in its awesome wonder and splendor, giving glory to God.

The final section focuses on Beatrice as teacher, mentor, and friend. John Shea provides a beautiful testimony of one whose own teaching and writings were deeply inspired by Bruteau. Carla DeSola chose Bruteau as her godmother after converting from Judaism to Catholicism. DeSola is a dancer and a teacher of dance and her essay describes in a unique and wonderful way how Bruteau's trinitarian theology of divine ecstatic love has influenced her ideas on dance and community. The closing essay is fittingly by Joshua Tysinger who accompanied Beatrice in the last months of her earthly life. His description of Beatrice as scholar, teacher and spiritual mother, while dining at the K and W cafeterias, incarnates this profound woman-scholar in a way that only personal experience could capture. Delightfully delineating her colloquialisms and unique mannerisms, Josh allows the reader to appreciate the real depth of this woman who wholeheartedly committed herself to the spontaneous bursting forth of new life, even as she suffered from the ravages of Alzheimer's disease in the last stages of her life.

Bruteau was one of those rare women who lived in the flowing streams of deep love, love she experienced in the living reality of God; in her husband, Jim Somerville; and in the many students and friends who sought her wisdom. She exemplifies the major contribution of women to theology in the twenty-first century and represents a new type of scholar, one free of the intellectual trappings of careerism. Philosopher, theologian, wife, spiritual mother, Beatrice Bruteau signals a new era for theology born out of the contemplative side of deep spirituality. She nurtures a new unity of theology and spirituality that does not negate philosophy but demands a new philosophical ground, which Teilhard described as a philosophy of love. A philosophy of love giving rise to the transformation of Neofeminine consciousness marks the deep insights of Beatrice Bruteau, whose work shines like a bright light on the new path of evolutionary spirituality. May we learn from her how to evolve into that creative freedom shown by Jesus, the freedom to do new things, a new level of consciousness where holiness is expressed in wholeness of life, and to realize we will never stop evolving for divine Love is always creating anew.

PART I

A DYNAMIC PERSON

You truly exist where you love,
not merely where you live.

—Bonaventure

1

Beatrice Bruteau

A Personal Memoir

Cynthia Bourgeault

Beatrice Bruteau—scholar, teacher, interspiritual pioneer, and intrepid explorer of the evolutionary edge of consciousness—quietly departed this earth plane on November 16, 2014, at the age of eighty-four. Her passing exemplified her signature brand of clarity, freedom, and intentionality, traits that for many decades had been hallmarks of her teaching presence among us.

I am still regularly surprised to discover, when I mention the name Beatrice Bruteau to Christian contemplative audiences, that the majority of those present have never heard of her. During her long and productive scholarly career she neither sought nor attained the "superstar" status now regularly conferred on the spiritual gurus of our times. By her own choice she preferred to remain slightly below the radar, where for nearly six decades she exerted her quiet presence as one of the most powerful influences on mystical theology, interspirituality, and contemplative practice.

This is a revised version of Cythia Bourgeault, "Interspiritual Pioneer Beatrice Bruteau Loomed Large in Comtemplative Universe," *National Catholic Reporter* (December 5–18, 2014).

Her two great passions were the meeting of East and West and the reconciliation of science and spirituality, particularly at their natural convergence point in the evolution of consciousness. In her lifetime she was a friend and colleague to such spiritual luminaries as Thomas Merton, Bede Griffiths, David Steindl-Rast, and many more of comparable stature, and a teacher to thousands of appreciative students, myself included. Those who had the privilege of working with her directly speak of the clarity and precision of her mind, the luminosity of her vision, and the down-to-earth practicality of her contemplative practice.

Beatrice Bruteau was born on July 25, 1930, in Carbondale, Illinois, and raised across the river in Jefferson City, Missouri. While her roots were solidly Midwestern and Baptist, her mother had a spiritually adventurous streak and was responsible for Beatrice's early exposure to the Vedanta tradition, which, at that time, was just beginning to percolate in the West. Her early career trajectory seemed headed toward mathematics, but while completing her master's degree at the University of Pittsburgh, she encountered the work of Aurobindo Ghose, and her world promptly turned upside down. She moved to New York City to study under Swami Pavitrananda, head of the Vedanta Society of New York, and later with the revered non-dual master Swami Nikhilanda. In short order she also began graduate studies in Philosophy at Fordham University (one of the first women admitted to the program) and received the PhD in 1954. Her dissertation, perhaps no surprise, was on Aurobindo, who remained a lifelong influence on her thought.

Despite her stellar academic credentials, Beatrice never pursued a permanent academic post. She taught regularly at Fordham, frequently in partnership with her former professor and Jesuit provincial James Somerville, SJ. But her interests clearly gravitated more toward opening up new lines of spiritual inquiry and conversation. Together with Somerville she founded the *American Philosophical Quarterly* in 1954 (by 1961 it had "morphed" into the distinguished *International Philosophical Quarterly*). She was a founding member of the Teilhard Society of America and founding director of the Teilhard Research Institute at Fordham.

During these Fordham years she also converted to Catholicism. While this may at first look like another major course shift, Beatrice was inwardly quite clear: "I didn't leave Vedanta; I carried it with me." As her long-time Vedanta colleague Swami Yogeshananda elaborated in a commemoration penned shortly after her death:

> Although deeply drawn to Vedanta and its exemplars, she ultimately decided that her role in the spiritual life was to attempt to carry the non-dual message into the very heart of the Christian witness. She was to be a Vedanta type Christian thinker. And thinker she was, stunning the academics of seminaries and theological schools with the brilliance of her penetration.[1]

In particular, her influence on two fellow Fordham graduates, Ewert Cousins and Ilia Delio, has revolutionized the playing field upon which the venerable intellectual tradition of Catholic Humanism is now unfolding.

On January 31, 1971, Beatrice and James Somerville married. (Her first husband, Fred Burkle, had died in 1970, and Jim had obtained release from the Jesuits.) Already committed spiritual partners, they now became partners in the fullest sense of the term in a remarkably devoted and spiritually generative marriage that would last for forty-four years. They departed New York City for Cincinnati, where Jim took up a new teaching post at Xavier University. Beatrice, meanwhile, continued to chart her course as an independent scholar, turning out two books that would shortly become foundational to the emerging fields of interspirituality and the evolution of consciousness: *Evolution toward Divinity*, her groundbreaking exploration of Teilhard

---

[1] "Tributes to Beatrice Bruteau," *American Vedantist* (Fall-Winter 2014–2015).

and Vedanta; and *The Psychic Grid*, by her own estimation her "breakthrough book" and personal favorite. With an eye to spiritual praxis as well as theory, Beatrice and Jim also launched a new publication, *The Contemplative Review* (1981).

In the mid-1980s they moved to Winston-Salem in order to be closer to Beatrice's ailing mother and brother. For the rest of her life Beatrice would call North Carolina her home. From her meticulously ordered home study she continued to write prodigiously, completing somewhere on the order of 150 articles and most of her major works, including *Radical Optimism* (1993), *The Easter Mysteries* (1995), *What We Can Learn from the East* (1995), and *God's Ecstasy: The Creation of a Self-Creating World* (1997). In all of these works she brought her deep understanding of non-dual states of consciousness, as well as her scientific training and rigor, to the mysticism of the West. She and Jim continued to edit *The International Philosophical Quarterly* and *The Contemplative Review* and helped launch *The American Vedantist* (1995).

In the spirit of "think globally, act locally," they also tended their vineyard at a much more grassroots level. Joining the local Episcopal church shortly after their arrival in Winston-Salem, they continued to build their *Schola Contemplationis* (School of Contemplation), originally created during their Cincinnati years, to address the growing spiritual hunger of the times. For more than thirty years they turned out their mind-bending monthly newsletter *The Roll* (produced on a home mimeograph machine and hand mailed to a small but devoted readership) in which Beatrice offered spiritual reflections and "trailers" of some of her most important work in progress. During the 1990s she and Jim also founded a local lay Benedictine Community called The Fellowship of the Holy Spirit. Meanwhile, she kept up her voluminous, worldwide spiritual correspondence and traveled regularly to Atlanta to offer retreats and to teach at the Atlanta Vedanta Center.

In her personal mannerisms she was decidedly "old school." She was dubious to the end about those newfangled inventions—email and the Internet—and never in her life did she set foot in an airplane. Her traveling range was limited by the distance she and Jim could cover in their grand old touring Cadillac (one of the thrills of her life was finally meeting Bede Griffiths face to face at a conference in New Harmony, Indiana, in 1983), and her preferred modes of communication were hands on, written and telephone, in that order. A Southern woman "to the nines," she dressed impeccably for every occasion and insisted that tea and coffee be served in proper china cups—never, heaven forbid, in mugs!

My own friendship with Beatrice Bruteau began in the late 1980s when I discovered her three-part article "Prayer and Identity" in the now-defunct *Contemplative Review* and had my spiritual universe quietly but completely overturned. Correspondence soon led to a personal visit and a mentoring relationship that would span the next three decades. I am honored to report that the very first public spiritual teaching I gave was at her behest, to her *Schola Contemplationis* group, in the early 1990s. In 2007 I was able in a small way to repay that gift when the *Sewanee Theological Review* invited me to republish her original "Prayer and Identity" article, together with a short commentary, in an issue dedicated to "Spirituality, Contemplation, and Transformation."

During this past decade our connection grew a bit more tenuous as my life got busier and hers gradually became more concentrated around that final stage of the journey, "growing into age." Around the fall of 2013 I began to hear rumors that Alzheimer's was starting to affect her magnificent brain, and in spring 2014, following a conference in Greensboro, I was able to pay her what turned out to be a final visit. While it was indeed obvious that the disease was making some inroads on the habitual operations along the horizontal axis of her life, as soon as we leaped into spiritual issues, her vast mind still took over like the lioness it was. Her teaching continued luminous and more and more vast.

Little did any of us at the time—maybe even Beatrice—suspect the final surprising denouement with which she would make her exit from this life. As it so happened, one of my younger students,

Joshua Tysinger, had begun his seminary studies at Wake Forest, right there in Winston-Salem, just about the time that Beatrice's life was rounding toward its finish. I suggested—and Josh was alert enough to follow up on the suggestion—that having a world-class spiritual master right in town was an opportunity not to be missed. He began to pay her regular visits, and it soon became clear that a lineage transmission was in process. As Josh willingly and sensitively helped Beatrice and Jim navigate the horizontal axis, her brilliant final imparting of a lifetime of spiritual wisdom and spiritual fire (mostly over lunch at the K &W Cafeteria, with, yes, proper coffee cups!) is an exchange that I suspect will not leave the planet unchanged.

I will leave this part of the story for Josh to tell in his own words when the right moment arises. For now, I would simply like to comment, from my own perspective, on what played out during the last three months of Beatrice's life. In late July she suffered a fall and was hospitalized and then in nursing care for several weeks. During this time it seemed that she was very much on the decline and "in transition." She ceased eating, and her already slight frame shrank to fifty pounds. By October a hospice worker had been called in, and Beatrice was seemingly hanging between the worlds.

Nine days before her death she sat up, got up, resumed eating enough to sustain the physical body a bit longer, and began to teach and transmit in a luminous burst of continuing insight. It was as if the Alzheimer's had been left behind—or perhaps, if truth be told, she had already "died" to this world and was returning, her own risen and Christed self in her imaginal body, to complete what was needed regarding this earth plane. While others were astonished at her sudden "improvement," she had already been extremely clear with Josh that this wasn't what it was about; it would be an entirely different dimension manifest in her. Teacher to the end, she left us with a luminous, stunningly hopeful demonstration of how a conscious death is already a Risen Life; the two are joined at the hip. With her final magnificent fusion of clarity, will, and freedom—all those qualities her spiritual practice had been about for more than half a century—

she went out like a bright candle, filling the whole room with the perfume of her realized being.

It is with great joy now that I join my voice with others whose lives she has so profoundly touched—particularly other spiritual *sisters,* for whom she serves as such a powerful inspiration and role model—to create this volume of essays in her honor.

PART II

PHILOSOPHER
AND THEOLOGIAN

*You are not a human being in search
of a spiritual experience.
You are a spiritual being immersed
in a human experience.*
—Pierre Teilhard de Chardin

2

Searching a Feminine Mystical Way for the Twenty-First Century

URSULA KING

Beatrice Bruteau was a most inspiring thinker who discovered Teilhard de Chardin's work early in the 1960s, soon after it had begun to be published. Her research at Fordham University was initially concerned with Sri Aurobindo,[1] but she soon became a close associate in setting up the American Teilhard de Chardin Association and also the Teilhard Research Institute at Fordham. In 1974, this interest in Teilhard led her to publish a comparative study on Teilhard and Aurobindo, *Evolution toward Divinity: Teilhard de Chardin and the Hindu Traditions.*[2]

This is an extensively revised version of my earlier article of the same title published in *Grace Jantzen—Redeeming the Present*, ed. Elaine L. Graham, 111–28 (Farnham: Ashgate, 2009). Used with permission of the publishers.

[1] See Beatrice Bruteau, *Worthy Is the World: The Hindu Philosophy of Sri Aurobindo* (Teaneck, NJ: Fairleigh Dickinson University, 1972).

[2] Beatrice Bruteau, *Evolution toward Divinity: Teilhard de Chardin and the Hindu Tradition* (Wheaton, IL: Theosophical Publishing House, 1974).

I first discovered Beatrice through this book and then followed her later publications with increasing interest. We corresponded a little, spoke on the phone in later years but, alas, never managed to meet, even though I tried, unsuccessfully, to arrange a visit to see her in North Carolina in 2005.

At the time of its publication Bruteau's comparative study on Teilhard and Aurobindo was the first of its kind. It stressed the similarities rather than the differences among traditional Indian thought and certain of its contemporary reinterpretations, such as that of Sri Aurobindo, with some of Teilhard's ideas. Bruteau points particularly to a common vision of God in the cosmos, God as energy, a similar approach to the problem of action, and the conquest of evil. Yet she unfortunately overlooked the fundamental difference in the understanding of evolution between Indian and Teilhardian thought, whereas he himself was fully aware of this. He clearly distinguished his own understanding of the evolutionary process, which included novelty, progressive growth, and ascent, from the Indian approach to evolution in terms of involution, whereby the Absolute, before evolving out of matter, first involved itself into it, so that evolution is understood as the gradual manifestation of what existed already. So there is nothing really new, no new being, and no real growth.

Bruteau's subsequent books show clearly that in her own thinking she worked with a thoroughly modern understanding of evolution that stresses the progressive dynamic of evolutionary becoming. To quote two examples, this finds a strong expression in *God's Ecstasy* (1997), where a whole chapter is titled "The Self-Creating Universe," and in *The Grand Option* (2001), where she invites her readers to enter into deep engagement with the "grand option" of creating a future linked to a new image of humanity animated by the spirit of love, both human and divine. In her "Tribute to Beatrice Bruteau," Cynthia Bourgeault has described her friend as an "interspiritual pioneer, and intrepid explorer of the evolutionary edge of consciousness" who was filled with spiritual wisdom and spiritual fire.[3]

---

[3] See Cynthia Bourgeault, "A Tribute to Beatrice Bruteau," *The Contemplative Society* (November 19, 2014).

I feel particularly inspired by Bruteau's chapter "Neo-Feminism and the Next Revolution in Consciousness" in *The Grand Option* and will briefly comment on it later in this chapter. Here, I want to raise a question that lies at the heart of this commemorative volume: can there be a feminine mystical way for the twenty-first century? In searching for an answer to this question, three different strands of reflection are pursued: (1) connecting mysticism and feminism; (2) exploring a *via feminina* for contemporary women and men; and (3) celebrating love, wisdom, and the feminine mystical way.

Connecting Mysticism and Feminism

Mysticism is difficult, if not impossible, to define. Many attempts have been made to understand this extraordinary religious phenomenon and its relationship to the larger context of religion. Although human reason remains ultimately unable to penetrate the mystery at the heart of mysticism, mystical experiences cannot be entirely opaque to reason and explanation either, as philosophers of religion have discussed at length.[4] The human spirit longs to reach out to something greater, more exalted and transcendent, to meet with and be transformed by the divine Spirit in the midst of life.

Mystics of many ages and faith communities bear supreme witness to the heights and depths of mystical experience. These mystics speak with many voices, they use a wealth of metaphors and images, and they have left us a bewildering range of narratives about their inner life and vision. Because of the great variety of mystical experiences it seems misleading to speak of mysticism in the singular. There are obviously many mysticisms, and numerous explanations have been offered by both mystics and scholars to account for what mysticism is all about. At one level the term *mysticism* seems rather artificial and undifferentiated; it seems

---

[4] See, for example, Grace M. Jantzen, "Could There Be a Mystical Core to Religion?" *Religious Studies* 26 (1990): 59–71; and especially idem, *Power, Gender, and Christian Mysticism* (Cambridge: Cambridge University Press, 1995).

more a word created by people studying, comparing, or talking about particular experiences that individual mystics themselves do not define as such. Mystics always speak about particular experiences, a particular faith or practice, a particular way or path, rather than about mysticism in general. Thus, being a mystic is very different from trying to understand what mysticism is, since it is about some of the most intimate and transformative spiritual experiences known to humankind.

More than thirty years ago I gave a lecture to an interfaith group in England entitled "Mysticism and Feminism *or* Why Look at Women Mystics?"[5] at a time when this was a relatively unheard-of topic. Some of my listeners on that occasion strongly objected on the grounds that mystical experience was beyond any feminist concerns. How can contemporary feminism as a social and political movement, but also a radical change in consciousness, be related to the age-old spiritual quest for liberation, freedom, enlightenment, and transcendence? Even with the more advanced gender-inclusive thinking of today, many people are unwilling to see that there is a deep connection between mysticism and feminism, beyond the obvious one that there have been many women mystics.

The literature on mysticism is vast and so is that on feminism. But comparatively few feminist theologians have written on mysticism, at least in comparison with all the other topics they have explored. Moreover, the leading authors on mysticism are still predominantly male and rarely use feminist insights or gender perspectives in their discussions of the subject. This has largely been left to a few women writers.

To most people who are not mystics themselves, mystical experience is only accessible through reading mystical literature. Such literature is found worldwide across different faiths and also outside them in a wide range of secular texts, consisting of the poetry and literature of many languages. When we examine their descriptions of spiritual experiences cross-culturally, certain

---

[5] *Teresa de Jesus and Her World*, ed. M. A. Rees, 7–17 (Leeds: Trinity and All Saints College, 1981).

common traits emerge. Central to them seems the insistence on a fundamental unity or oneness that transcends all the diversity, fragmentation, and superficiality of daily life. Thus, mysticism has often been defined as a fundamentally unitive experience. In Christianity and other theistic religions this is understood as the deepest love and communion with God, whereas non-theistic religions conceive of it as a deeply contemplative approach to Ultimate Reality. Union, contemplation, love, and bliss all feature in the description of mystical experiences. Beatrice Bruteau also emphasizes that mysticism has above all to do with "unitary consciousness," which she describes as "a state of consciousness in which <u>one grasps in a global way the unity of all one knows—one's whole world.</u> . . . But usually the term is restricted to the unmediated experience of ground-level consciousness as Ground of Being."[6]

It comes as something of a surprise to realize that the *comparative* study of mysticism—as distinct from the existence of mystics of many faiths—dates only from the beginning of the twentieth century, whether one thinks of William James's famous *Varieties of Religious Experience* (1902) or Evelyn Underhill's equally famous study entitled *Mysticism: The Nature and Development of Spiritual Consciousness* (1911). Many other authors and titles could be mentioned here. The rediscovery of many women mystics of the past occurred also mainly during the twentieth century. This rediscovery has by no means been the exclusive achievement of women, yet it is striking how many women scholars have made important contributions to the modern study of mysticism.

Contemporary historical, theological, and comparative studies on mysticism still pay relatively scant attention to wider gender issues. Nor do they always give sufficient space to women mystics. However, this does now happen more frequently since the works of many women mystics in Christianity, Islam, Hinduism, and other religions have been discovered or rediscovered since

---

[6] Beatrice Bruteau, *God's Ecstasy: The Creation of a Self-Creating World* (New York: Crossroad, 1997), 193.

the last century. Many women scholars have done significant work on the historical, textual, and descriptive study of mysticism, without necessarily being attentive to gender issues. To mention some names besides Evelyn Underhill, there are Margaret Smith, Geraldine Hodgson, Phyllis Hodgson, Hope Emily Allen, Emily Herman, Hilda Graef, and, more recently, Annemarie Schimmel, Grace Jantzen, and many others. These have all written extensively on mysticism, and sometimes specifically on women mystics.

The relationship between mysticism and feminism is ambivalent and rather difficult to unpack. From a critical feminist perspective many questions can be asked. What have been women's own religious experiences in the past as distinct from those of men? How far have women articulated their experiences differently? Have they used different metaphors, concepts, and images of their own? To what extent are their accounts more personal and autobiographical? How do they claim authority for their words and visions, and what writing strategies did they adopt to be accepted by their contemporaries?

The mystical writings of women in the past were often not acknowledged in the official historiographies of religious institutions; nor did they contribute to the systematic articulations of faith created in theological and philosophical schools of learning. Thus, many works by women mystics have long remained invisible and marginalized as, for example, Julian of Norwich's important *Showings*.

Much has been written on medieval women mystics, yet relatively few writers combine the insights of the mystical tradition with the critical insights of contemporary feminism. Although "women of spirit" of earlier ages have sometimes been called "proto-feminists," many aspects of their life and thinking relate very little to ours. Medieval women mystics were certainly not feminists in any contemporary sense. Their work, therefore, has to be approached with caution. Much of it remains imprisoned in the patriarchal framework of past hierarchical structures and thinking.

Every religion knows of female saints and mystics—extraordinary women who have provided much spiritual counsel, guidance, and largely noninstitutionalized spiritual leadership, just as Julian did from her cell in Norwich. It comes as no surprise that such "women of spirit," women who possessed spiritual power or what Eleanor McLaughlin has called the "power out of holiness,"[7] greatly appeal to people today who are seeking spiritual guidance and inspiration. Religious women of medieval and early modern times provide strong role models in terms of female identity, autonomous agency, and inner strength in face of much social and religious opposition. The comparative study of the writings of female and male mystics from a perspective of gender differences raises searching questions, not least for contemporary religious practice and the development of an appropriate, viable spirituality for both genders in our globalized society.

A surprising development worldwide is the growing realization of the global spiritual heritage of women across different religions and cultures. Many spiritual "foremothers," female saints, mystics, and female religious communities are being discovered today. Yet a comparative historical enquiry provides plenty of evidence that most religions have validated women's lives primarily in terms of domestic observances and family duties. Religions have been less inclined to encourage women's search for religious experience and enlightenment, or to follow exceptional paths of spiritual devotion and perfection. Imprisoned by the daily tasks and recurrent demands of immediacy that the maintenance and nurture of personal and community life have always required, women have been so much equated with *immanence* that the realms of *transcendence* have remained largely out of their reach, forbidden to their desire.

In spite of the existence of what German theologian Elisabeth Gössmann calls "women's counter-tradition" to official

---

[7] Eleanor McLaughlin, "Women, Power, and the Pursuit of Holiness," in *Women of Spirit: Female Leadership in the Jewish and Christian Traditions*, ed. Rosemary Ruether and E. McLaughlin (New York: Simon and Schuster, 1979), 100–130. I have discussed this and the relationship between mysticism and feminism at greater length in "Voices of Spiritual Power," chapter 4 in *Women and Spirituality: Voices of Protest and Promise*, 2nd ed. (London: Macmillan, 1993).

Christianity,[8] pursuing the life of the spirit always remained an exceptional path open mainly to individual women from an advantaged social background. We therefore have to ask how far women really have had access to a spiritual space of their own? How far have they been encouraged to pursue or have been admitted to the pursuit of similar spiritual ideals and disciplines as men or, even more important from our perspective, how far did (a few) women possess the necessary freedom to develop their own spirituality? How far could women provide spiritual advice and leadership for both women and men?

It is only in our postmodern era that women *as a group,* and not simply as individuals, have been able to respond in greater numbers to the invitation, challenge, and gift of *transcendence.* That raises questions about modern women mystics and the possibility of developing a feminine mystical way in the twenty-first century.

Exploring a *Via Feminina* for Contemporary Women and Men

It is not my task here to review the critical feminist literature on women mystics or on the feminine in Christian mysticism, but I want to refer briefly to a few helpful titles. Grace Jantzen's *Power, Gender, and Christian Mysticism* (1995) is of great importance and has attracted much attention, but its full discussion would require another essay. Equally important is Barbara Newman's excellent analysis *Sister of Wisdom* (1987),[9] which examines the feminine motifs and the theology of the feminine in Hildegard of Bingen. An earlier, pioneering feminist study on Teresa of Avila

---

[8] Elisabeth Gössmann, "The Image of God and the Human Being in Women's Counter-Tradition," in *Is There a Future for Feminist Theology?* ed. Deborah F. Sawyer and Diane M. Collier, 26–56 (Sheffield: Sheffield Academic Press, 1999).

[9] Barbara Newman, *Sister of Wisdom: St. Hildegard's Theology of the Feminine* (Berkeley and Los Angeles: University of California Press, 1987).

and the Western mystical tradition is Deidre Green's book *Gold in the Crucible* (1989),[10] still worth reading, especially for its concluding reflections entitled "Teresa and the Issue of Women's Spirituality." Far more theoretically nuanced, but quite difficult, is Amy Hollywood's more recent study *Sensible Ecstasy* (2002).[11] It draws on the psychological theories of Luce Irigaray and Jacques Lacan in its discussion of medieval mystics, and of mysticism and gender. Amy Hollywood also highlights the distinction between affective or erotic forms of mysticism, usually associated with women, and the more speculative, intellectual forms of mysticism, usually associated with men. Another way of saying this is to align *apophatic* mysticism and negative theology with male intellectual speculations, whereas *kataphatic* forms of mysticism, associated with imagery, symbolism, and affirmative forms of theology, are more frequently linked with women mystics.

I have been particularly inspired by the approach of another contemporary writer, Beverly Lanzetta, who published a daring, innovative book entitled *Radical Wisdom: A Feminist Mystical Theology*, and the study *Emerging Heart: Global Spirituality and the Sacred*. More recently, she has published the stunning account of her own mystical journey, *Nine Jewels of Night: One Soul's Journey into God*, followed by the *Path of the Heart: A Spiritual Guide to Divine Union*. In seeking a feminine mystical way for the twenty-first century, it is worth listening to Lanzetta's ideas, some of which I want to share here.[12]

Beverly Lanzetta is convinced of the importance of gender implications for the spiritual life. She invites us to a rereading of

---

[10] Deidre Green, *Gold in the Crucible: Teresa of Avila and the Western Mystical Tradition* (Shaftesbury: Element Books, 1989).

[11] Amy Hollywood, *Sensible Ecstasy* (Chicago: University of Chicago Press, 2002).

[12] Beverly Lanzetta, *Radical Wisdom: A Feminist Mystical Theology* (Minneapolis: Fortress Press, 2005); idem, *Emerging Heart: Global Spirituality and the Sacred* (Minneapolis: Fortress Press, 2007); idem, *Nine Jewels of Night: One Soul's Journey into God* (San Diego: Blue Sapphire Books, 2014); idem, *Path of the Heart: A Spiritual Guide to Divine Union* (San Diego: Blue Sapphire Books, 2015).

mystical theology from a feminist angle in order to discover new spiritual lineages and revelatory traditions. Just as Sara Maitland argued long ago that we need women mapmakers of the interior country,[13] so Lanzetta too speaks of women standing on the borders of a new country as mapmakers of uncharted spiritual territory. She asks: "What metaphors, symbols, images of God do women see, unite with, and reveal if they travel by the way of the feminine? What wisdom can be gleaned from medieval women mystics on the geography of the soul?"[14] She deliberately speaks of the *via feminina,* a feminine way not restricted to women but open to both women and men, although it expresses itself differently in females than in males. She means by this feminine way a quality of religious consciousness and a mystical path that tread new ground. Thus, she redefines the spiritual journey from the perspective of women, but not in an exclusive sense. Instead of seeking union with God through either the *via positiva* or the *via negativa,* she sees the *via feminina,* the feminine mystical way, as a "third way," unveiling to us "the feminine heart of divinity and the spiritual equality of women."[15] She presents the *via feminina* as a "radical mysticism" that seeks new forms of expression and engagement, while recognizing at the same time that some features of traditional mysticism reveal themselves as products of patriarchy. These have to be dismantled and replaced by something new for the present world.

Beverly Lanzetta's feminist mystical theology develops with the full awareness that much of past mystical thinking requires deconstruction. She writes: "If mysticism traces the journey to freedom, then women cannot achieve their full spiritual potential without confronting the injustice and violence within which the terms *female-feminine-woman* have been inscribed throughout recorded history."[16]

---

[13] See Sara Maitland, *A Map of the New Country: Women and Christianity* (London: Routledge, Kegan Paul, 1983).

[14] Lanzetta, *Radical Wisdom,* 8.

[15] Ibid., 13.

[16] Ibid., 16.

She addresses the historical subservice of women in theological and spiritual circles, and she critiques the still prevalent prohibition against women in the highest spheres of spiritual authority and the still rampant oppression of women in religious institutions. However, beyond this critique or the "un-saying" of "woman" as traditionally understood—deconstructing and un-saying all that falsely defines "woman" and "feminine"[17]— and the elimination of all forms of oppression, the *via feminina* moves on as a path of spiritual liberation. This includes a dynamic relationship between embodiment and transcendence. It pays particular attention to the multiple wisdom of body, psyche, and soul in order to name and heal what diminishes or violates women.

> Its single most distinguishing feature is that as a spiritual path it does not transcend differences—whether of gender, culture, race, or sex—but enters into them directly to experience a deeper unity capable of transforming the underlying causes of soul suffering. . . . [*Via feminina*] is vigilant about the ways in which the categories that name and define the spiritual life—redemption, salvation, soul, self, God, virtue—as well as the processes or stages of mystical ascent—purgation, dark night, union—repeat subtle forms of gender, racial, or social violence.[18]

Lanzetta's reflections emerge out of her experience as a spiritual director as well as her role as a scholar. The depth and richness of her work invite numerous rereadings, much critical reflection and engaging debate. If I understand Lanzetta correctly, she seeks to dismantle "the great lie about the feminine"[19] in her trenchant critique of some of the oppressive aspects of traditional mysticism and spirituality. This is especially so when she speaks with much sensitivity and wisdom about women's spiritual oppression and wounding, and their great need for healing. She

---

[17] Ibid., 24.
[18] Ibid., 22.
[19] Ibid., 17.

understands intimately what it means "to experience the wound of being female in this world."[20] By way of critique it must be mentioned, however, that Lanzetta unfortunately ignores the central issues of power and authority, so carefully analyzed in Grace Jantzen's *Power, Gender, and Christian Mysticism.*

On the constructive side, Lanzetta suggests a wholesome, integral, embodied, and undivided spirituality that is desirable, helpful, and healing for both women and men. She characterizes the feminine mystical way *(via feminina)* as "a socially engaged and bodily contemplative practice" that will assist "in the expansion and refinement of a spirituality that is truly representative of our global, changing, and pluralistic world."[21]

It is particularly exciting to see how in charting the *via feminina* as a partly new way, Lanzetta draws support from the experiences of medieval women mystics, especially Julian of Norwich and Teresa of Avila. Both are presented as "cartographers of the soul" and "sisters in spirit" who stand out through their wise and mature guidance. Both women share spiritual lives and theologies that resonate remarkably with each other. Both traveled from female subordination to dignity and freedom:

> As marginalized females in predominately male-dominated cultures, it was through their contemplative experiences and prayerful dialogues with God that they worked out their personal wounding and social concerns. In their struggles toward spiritual equality they mapped out an inner feminism—the territory of the soul by which mysticism becomes the site of women's empowerment and dignity.[22]

Lanzetta describes Julian's mystical experience as "graphic and raw," especially when Julian contemplates the thirsting face and crucified body of Jesus on the cross. She recognizes Julian's distinctive theology of the feminine, "in which the meaning of sin and

---

[20] Ibid., 135.
[21] Ibid., 24.
[22] Ibid., 83.

suffering is transformed and her worth as a woman is affirmed. Conceptualizing this journey through the image of the mother-hood of God, Julian works out her equality and dignity of personhood, and the sinlessness of her fellow Christians."[23] Lanzetta affirms our need for a feminine Divine, our longing to experience God as mother, as Julian does so movingly when she speaks about God and Jesus as our mother and praises God's all-embracing motherly love for the whole of creation again and again.

Some of Lanzetta's views on the *via feminina* are not unlike what Beatrice Bruteau writes in "Neo-Feminism and the Next Revolution in Consciousness" in *The Grand Option*.[24] She criticizes there the polarity of feminine and masculine consciousness, which can be transcended through the development of a new holistic and *participatory consciousness*. This is characterized by (1) a consciousness of the whole, concrete, real person; (2) establishing identity though mutual affirmation rather than negation; and (3) perceiving being existentially rather than essentially.[25]

Others may refer to the development of this new consciousness as an evolutionary consciousness. Bruteau seems to agree with this when she points to our intense involvement with the sense of the future and says that "we are self-conscious evolution," experiencing "another turn in the evolutionary spiral."[26] Bruteau expresses and inspires great hope when she concludes so expectantly:

> We already feel we are the people of the future, people of a great frontier whose borders are unknown. We know that it has not yet appeared what shall be. . . . We ourselves *are* the future and we *are* the revolution. If and when the next revolution comes, it will come as *we* turn and the world turns with us.[27]

---

[23] Ibid., 84.

[24] Bruteau, *The Grand Option*, 17–32.

[25] Ibid., 26.

[26] Ibid., 18.

[27] Ibid., 32.

Much more could be said on this, but I move on in order to reflect on the place of love and wisdom, so much needed for healing our deep spiritual wounds today. They form a distinctive part of a feminine mystical way that can help us to renew contemporary spirituality.

Celebrating Love, Wisdom, and the Feminine Mystical Way

Counselors, pastors, even some politicians, and many ordinary people are all well aware of the great spiritual hunger that reveals itself in so many ways in the contemporary world. What can be done to bring about more justice, harmony, peace, and happiness in a world so deeply torn apart, where so many people suffer great material, emotional, and spiritual deprivation?

Countless individuals, groups of activists, and institutions wrestle with these questions. Numerous suggestions and plans have been developed. Some religious thinkers have proposed a global ethic; others speak of the need for global meditation but also global action to change the world together for the better. Beverly Lanzetta comes up with the excellent idea of recognizing distinctive *spiritual rights* that build upon international human rights. This brings a new perspective to global suffering, including women's suffering, since spiritual rights ask us "to see each other and all creation from a divine perspective," with God's eyes, so to speak. She writes:

> Because the highest calling of the person is to have fullness of being, spiritual rights address what prevents or violates this pursuit. As the common element in all human cultures and traditions, the spiritual dimension of life is intertwined with and underlies all other rights. . . . It recognizes that spirituality is life itself; thus, a life of dignity is inconceivable without spiritual integrity and freedom. . . . Derived from a belief that recognizes within other people the presence of the divine through which a person

attains full humanity, spiritual rights place the expressly spiritual as a recognized right interdependent with and interrelated to civil and political rights, and economic and social rights.[28]

I find the notion of spiritual rights a very helpful one, although it needs further elaboration. The inclusion of spiritual rights into the vocabulary of rights enables us to think about human dignity from a different perspective. It also reminds us that mental and spiritual violence as well as physical violence can destroy not only the human body but also the human spirit. In Lanzetta's words, spiritual rights are "attentive to a certain quality of consciousness and a certain depth of heart that heal and transform. An indivisible relationship exists between the attainment of planetary responsibility and the necessity for spiritual practices, prayer, and meditative solitude."[29]

The distinctiveness of spiritual rights leads Lanzetta to an "ethic of ultimate concern," an embodied engagement that moves out of contemplation into action in the human sphere and into love for the world. She calls this a "mystical ethic," which she describes as "in essence, a mothering one; it embraces the world as a mother's body surrounds and nurtures life within her womb. Metaphors of pregnancy and birth help convey how each day we bear—lay our bodies down for—the spiritual renewal of life."[30]

As human beings we are not only responsible for attention to our own selfhood, or for what happens to our family, friends, and neighbors. As a morally and spiritually evolving species we also carry a common responsibility for the human family around the globe. For this we need to learn to nurture much more the qualities of love and wisdom than we have done hitherto by being attentive to spiritual energy resources as well as material

---

[28] Lanzetta, *Radical Wisdom*, 183.

[29] Ibid., 184

[30] Ibid., 197.

ones. Thus, we have to learn to recognize God's love in our lives and respond to it by accepting ourselves and loving others. It also means that we have much work to do to transform ourselves and our material culture that is so "blinded to the unseen."[31]

To quote another modern Christian mystic, Pierre Teilhard de Chardin, "The day will come when humanity, after harnessing the energies of space, winds, water, and gravity, will harness the energies of love for God—and on that day humans, for the second time in the history of the world, will have discovered fire."[32] The transformative power of love is well captured in another of Teilhard's sayings: "Love is the free and imaginative outpouring of the spirit over all unexplored paths."[33] Like other mystics, Teilhard affirms that without this all-transforming power of love and the zest for life, human development at an individual and social level cannot be sustained.

It is remarkable how many similar ideas about the spiritual energy resources of love and wisdom are emerging among different individuals and groups around the globe. Contemporary thought in the sciences and arts, in religion and psychology, in psychotherapy and counseling, in human development and social thinking, provide many examples of this convergence of similarly conceived ideals for the human community. It is not only mystics, theologians, and novelists who wrestle with love. Today, whole research groups and projects are devoted to this topic. They are trying to find out what difference personal and altruistic love can make to the life of human beings in terms of health, happiness, joy, and contentment.

A striking instance of some powerful parallel but entirely independent thinking about the transformative power of love is found in the writings of Pierre Teilhard de Chardin (1881–1955) and the magisterial study *The Ways and Power of Love* by

---

[31] Ibid., 173.

[32] Pierre Teilhard de Chardin, *Toward the Future,* trans. René Hague (London: Collins, 1975), 87.

[33] Pierre Teilhard de Chardin, *The Future of Man,* trans. Norman Denny (London: Collins, 1964), 55.

Russian-American sociologist Pitirim A. Sorokin (1889–1968),[34] founding professor of sociology at Harvard University. Both consider altruistic love the highest human energy resource for the transformation of human society. Both also agree that humans at present know less about "love energy" than about the different forms of physical energy such as light, heat, and electricity. The transformative energies of love must be studied in all their different dimensions, whether cosmic, physical, biological, psychological, social, religious, or ethical. Sorokin speaks of love as one of the highest energies known to human beings. Like Teilhard, he thinks that the production and distribution of love have until now been given little systematic thought in practically all societies. This shows an astounding lack of organized effort on the part of humanity—or, one might say, a lack of spiritual focus and depth—and this lack now threatens humanity's very future. Throughout history the family has been one of the most efficient agencies in producing altruistic love, and so have small religious communities, saints, and mystics, but altruistic love must now be extended beyond these small groups to the human "world market," according to Sorokin.[35] He paints a bold picture of the transformative power of love and the systematic possibility of developing, accumulating, and storing its energy for the benefit of individuals and communities. The great geniuses, heroes, and apostles of love throughout history, including the mystics, are like "great power stations producing love for generations of human beings."[36] But their example alone is not enough. What is needed now is an increase of love production by ordinary people and groups, in fact, by the whole culture, so that "love, radiated by culture and by social institutions, would form a permanent

---

[34] Pitirim A. Sorokin, *The Ways and Power of Love: Types, Factors, and Techniques of Moral Transformation* (Philadelphia: Templeton Foundation, 2002; 1st ed. 1954). A more detailed discussion of this convergence of thought is found in Ursula King, "Love—A Higher Form of Human Energy in the Work of Teilhard de Chardin and Sorokin," *Zygon: Journal of Religion and Science* 39/1 (2004): 77–102.

[35] Sorokin, *The Ways and Power of Love*, 39.

[36] Ibid., 40.

atmosphere that would pervade all human beings from the cradle to the grave."[37]

Is this merely a utopian dream or is it possible to work for such change? For this to happen, a global *spiritual awakening* has to occur. This requires *spiritual education* at all levels, not only for children and young people but as an integral part of lifelong adult learning. Only then can we achieve what I call *spiritual literacy*, a literacy that goes beyond learning to read and write, beyond emotional and ethical literacy, to a much deeper dimension of insight and wisdom that grows from the heart and fosters compassion and love.

Learning to love differently, following the rise of evolutionary consciousness and becoming, is an urgent task. We need deeply transformative ideas for this, as suggested by Bruteau, Lanzetta, Teilhard, Sorokin, and many other contemporary thinkers and spiritual practitioners. To highlight such deeply inspiring and transforming ideas, which can extend our sensibilities, nurture spiritual awakening, and foster a greater spiritual literacy in contemporary society, I have suggested the use of the word *pneumatophore*.[38] Originally drawn from the taxonomy of the plant kingdom, this term carries a profound ecological meaning. Botanists use it to refer to the air roots of plants growing in swampy waters. Such roots, sticking out into the air, are carriers of *pneuma*, of air or spirit, if this word is translated literally. When I first used the word during a public lecture, one of the people present understood this word as "new metaphor." This is not inappropriate, since *pneumatophore* is meant to be used metaphorically in my reflections, in the sense that I understand it as referring to those transformative, empowering ideas and inspirations that can serve as bearers of spirit and channels for new life of individuals and communities today.

---

[37] Ibid., 45.

[38] I have drawn here on my essay "Pneumatophores for Nurturing a Different Kind of Love," in *Through Us, with Us, in Us: Relational Theologies in the Twenty-First Century*, ed. Lisa Isherwood and Elaine Bellchambers, 52–70 (London: SCM Press, 2010), where these ideas are more fully discussed.

Within the secularity of modern society we need many such *pneumatophores,* ideas that are vibrant bearers of spirit, ideas that can literally "inspire" and guide us to generate new life and develop a deeper, more unitary mystical consciousness. Such ideas may be drawn from traditional religions, secular society, the sciences, or the arts; they may arise from the sacred or the secular, from national, transnational, or global contexts. It does not matter where they come from as long as they lead us to a heightened awareness and sensibility, a sense of global responsibility, and a new kind of spiritual literacy that can help people to live a life of dignity on the planet and develop a new consciousness of the oneness of the earth and all its peoples. The idea of a new kind of love is one such idea, and so is the idea of wisdom.

The figure of wisdom—*sapientia* or *sophia*—has played a central role in the theologies of the feminine in different historical periods. This is true of medieval times, when Hildegard of Bingen has been called "sister of wisdom"[39] and Julian has been described as "wisdom's daughter." Julian herself says that "God all wisdom is our loving Mother."[40] There has been a modern revival of sapiential theology, from the Romantics to Eastern Orthodox thinkers like Soloviev, Bulgakov, and Florensky, but also in Teilhard de Chardin, with his poem "The Eternal Feminine."[41] Over the centuries both men and women have been attracted to such theologies of the feminine. In Barbara Newman's view, "these systems of thought cannot be explained solely by women's alleged need to identify with powerful feminine symbols, or by men's purported need to project these symbols as images of

---

[39] For a discussion of sapiential theologies, feminism, and the future, see Newman, *Sister of Wisdom,* chap. 7. See also Joan Nuth, *Wisdom's Daughter: The Theology of Julian of Norwich* (New York: Crossroad, 1991).

[40] Julian of Norwich, chap. 58, in Grace M. Jantzen, *Julian of Norwich: Mystic and Theologian* (Mahwah, NJ: Paulist Press, 2000), 111.

[41] See "The Eternal Feminine," in Pierre Teilhard de Chardin, *Writings in Time of War,* trans. René Hague, 191–202 (London: Collins, 1968).

desire."[42] Thus, symbols of the feminine, of the figure of Wisdom, and indeed of a feminine Divine, may be addressing the psychological needs of both women and men. Yet, explanations of how they came about and what may be the meaning of these symbols for people's lives today vary enormously, from psycholinguistic theories, to social and political explanations, to a variety of philosophical and theological perspectives. Wisdom as Sophia plays an important role in feminist spirituality and theology. Yet, it is not only Wisdom as female representation of the Divine, but women's own wisdom that has found new recognition today.

Thomas Berry describes the wisdom of women as one of four essential resources for contemporary cultural and spiritual renewal. He sees "the great work" of building a viable future for people and planet as a human project that belongs to both women and men. However, it demands the transformation of all our institutions, from global politics, governance, education, and financial arrangements to all aspects of culture, including religion. Berry thinks that humankind will not be able to achieve this radical transformation if we do not draw on all available resources. Most important among these are four kinds of wisdom: that of indigenous peoples, that of women, that of the classical philosophical and religious traditions of the world, and the new wisdom of science (sometimes called by him "the Yoga of the West"), still in its beginning phase, but advancing with amazing speed and success. The wisdom of women is very ancient, but it is now reasserting itself in new forms, transforming Western and other civilizations. Berry says, "The wisdom of women is to join the knowing of the body to that of mind, to join soul to spirit, intuition to reasoning, feeling consciousness to intellectual analysis, intimacy to detachment, subjective presence to objective distance."[43] This can be read as a description of some of the qualities associated with a feminine mystical way that is now open to both women and men and is prefigured in the lives of earlier women mystics.

---

[42] Newman, *Sister of Wisdom*, 266.

[43] Thomas Berry, *The Great Work: Our Way into the Future* (New York: Bell Tower, 1999), 180.

The American Dominican Father Richard Woods has explored the similarity between the experiences of medieval and modern women mystics, perceiving their liberating, even revolutionary, force and prophetic function. He also recognizes with much discernment that

> women today are accomplishing what women in the Middle Ages sought to achieve in their own time—they are redefining the sense of God as a supportive presence not only favourable toward women (as well as men), but as a spirit of liberation from the fear, disdain, prejudice, stereotypes, and active discrimination that has characterised men's attitudes towards women throughout much of the modern era and in many, perhaps most areas of the world. . . . With regard to their position in the Christian church in particular, women are protesting against their disenfranchisement as children to one God, co-heirs with Christ, full members of the Body of Christ, and adult citizens of the Reign of God, the heavenly City. They are doing so not only by pressing for full incorporation into ministry, but, as happened with Augustinian canonesses, Hildegard, the Cistercian nuns, the beguines, and even Julian of Norwich, establishing havens or sanctuaries where they are free to express their spirituality and . . . to mature personally and collectively. . . .
>
> Emancipation and liberation are not themselves the goal of mystical experience. And yet, paradoxically, it is for that reason that it attains them.[44]

Conclusion

Theologians like Karl Rahner and William Johnston can only see a future for Christianity, the church, or even religion, if

---

[44] Father Richard Woods, OP, *Mediaeval and Modern Women Mystics: The Evidential Character of Religious Experience*, Second Series of Occasional Papers 7 (Lampeter: Religious Experience Research Centre, August 1997), 19–20.

mysticism and mystical spirituality take the lead in people's lives. The contribution of women mystics and the further emergence of a feminine mystical way that embraces the powers of love and wisdom are indispensable for this.

It is not all that long ago that the great contemporary interest in Julian of Norwich's *Showing of Love*[45] first took off. In earlier centuries Walter Hilton, Richard Rolle, and the *Cloud of Unknowing* were much better known than Julian of Norwich. It was those men who were then considered typical "English mystics," whereas now it is Julian of Norwich who seems to be the best known of all the English medieval mystics. Maybe we are moving into the age of the feminine in two different senses.

First, in spite of the ongoing oppression and violence toward women and continuing gender disparity we have to recognize that women in the West, but increasingly also globally, have achieved much material advancement in the social, economic, legal, and educational sphere. But it is also part of women's calling to gain full equality and authority in the spiritual sphere by developing a new *spiritual literacy* whereby women define religion and spirituality for themselves rather than being passively defined by them. This is now happening in all religions, although the pace of change may differ widely. But this radical shift among women and religion is so little generally known that it has been described as a silent revolution going on around the world.

Second, given the global rise in women's general and spiritual literacy, it is not surprising that women are developing new approaches to spirituality that combine the insights of faith and feminism. That includes various attempts to develop a more inclusive feminine mystical way, a new "radical wisdom" that embraces an embodied and actively engaged contemplation nurtured by a mystical ethic "enfolded in love," as suggested by Beverly Lanzetta and others.

---

[45] Julian of Norwich, *Showing of Love: Extant Texts and Translation,* ed. Sister Anna Maria Reynolds, CP, and Julia Bolton Holloway (Florence: SISMEL, Edizioni del Galluzzo, 2001; Collegeville, MN: Liturgical Press, 2003).

Spiritual work is demanding, not light work; its benefits cannot be gained without effort. To lead women and men of today to spiritual awakening and a deeper awareness, to a new spiritual consciousness and an actively engaged spiritual practice, is the great calling of our time. It demands many spiritual resources. It requires great integrity, deep honesty and truthfulness, and a passionate commitment to the life of the Spirit, to become "attuned to the rivers of longing that flow between the divine and human heart.[46] The women mystics of the past, but even more the mystical writers of the present, such as Beatrice Bruteau, Beverly Lanzetta, and others, can help us carve a new mystical way commensurate with a new consciousness at a new stage of evolutionary transformation.

---

[46] Lanzetta, *Radical Wisdom*, 87.

3

Personal and Cultural Maturation

A Revolution in Consciousness

Barbara Fiand, SNDdeN

We are inescapably creators of [our] future in the most fundamental sense of determining the basic value patterns of
perception that order all our other experiences and thereby
compose our human "world." None of us can renounce our
freedom or flee our consciousness. Neither can we avoid
making ourselves, one another, and our world to be as we
and it shall be. . . . We ourselves *are* the future and we *are*
the revolution.[1]

This is how Beatrice Bruteau concluded her essay "Neo-
Feminism and the Next Revolution of Consciousness," first published in *Anima* in 1977. In the early 1980s a colleague of mine
shared this essay with me as I was teaching a course in Christian

---

[1] Beatrice Bruteau, *The Grand Option: Personal Transformation
and a New Creation* (Notre Dame, IN: University of Notre Dame Press,
2001), 32.

43

anthropology at that time and was keenly interested in theories addressing personal and cultural maturation. I had been working with the thoughts of Bernard J. Boelen pertaining to individual transformation[2] that seemed to my colleague to parallel what Beatrice Bruteau was addressing on the broader cultural level.

Bruteau's contribution to the whole field of consciousness transformation immediately absorbed me. I was especially fascinated by her emphasis on the word *revolution,* since it so clearly points to the enormity and profundity of the "rearrangement in our life experience" that challenges our future. As Bruteau insists: "A genuine revolution must be a gestalt shift in the whole way of seeing our relations to one another so that our behavior patterns are reformed from the inside out."[3] She sees us as "self-conscious evolution" spiraling upward or outward toward ever-higher and wider levels of consciousness that, nevertheless, are built on, and eventually incorporate, beneficial aspects of the preceding ones. It must be stressed that this is not an automatic transformative event of which we passively receive what is new. That is why the word *revolution* is so important. Our response is important, even though we do not know precisely what lies ahead as we move toward its emergence. Although Bruteau surmises that the stage of consciousness that we are moving toward at the present time will very likely be strikingly different from the one immediately preceding it, she believes that some basic resemblance with earlier levels seems highly possible due to the spiraling nature of

---

[2] Bernard J. Boelen is retired professor of philosophy at De Paul University in Chicago. He earned the PhD from the University of Louvain and then was associated with many institutions of higher learning in the United States as well as in Europe. He is most widely known for his book *Existential Thinking: A Philosophical Orientation,* which is best described as "a systematic re-thinking of philosophy out of the primordial phenomenon of wonder as its starting point and its lasting source of inspiration" (Duquesne University Press). His *Personal Maturity: The Existential Dimension* is a "broad and humanistic vision of the fully integrated person" (Continuum). Boelen has lectured extensively both in academic settings and to the broader public.

[3] Bruteau, *The Grand Option,* 17.

this entire movement that at all times circles back on itself, even if at a higher and more advanced level.

Level One in Personal Maturation

I am especially drawn to Bruteau's theory of self-conscious evolution because the possibilities I see when connecting it to Boelen's model for personal maturation are profound. It is clear that cultures and those who belong to them are inextricably one. As we study the two theories in tandem, therefore, rather than separately, our *personal* responsibility for the evolutionary spiraling of cultural consciousness can be highlighted and intensified. Human beings, after all, are the "freedom," the fundamental openness, and as the mystics would have it, the essentially "empty space" where evolutionary consciousness can happen. We are, in Martin Heidegger's way of thinking, the place where "Being" lights up, where everything that is can find meaning. In us also, according to Teilhard de Chardin, the love that empowers evolution can be consciously and freely acknowledged and embraced. We are the potential and the actualization of consciousness as it evolves. We are openness in process.

For Bernard Boelen there are, so far, three levels of human maturation and the quest for meaning associated with each level.[4] Each is nuanced by a number of sublevels.[5] The movement from one level of awareness to another is not at all easy. It can perhaps best be described as a turning point or crisis, intensely and often painfully experienced and occasionally resisted, even as the inner drive for meaning urges us toward new ways of

---

[4] Being an existential thinker and phenomenologist, Boelen leaves open the possibility of further levels that are yet totally unknown and therefore even beyond conjecture.

[5] The scope of this chapter and its purpose does not permit a detailed discussion of the sublevels in each stage of conscious evolution. I refer the interested reader to Boelen's *Personal Maturity;* for a simpler version, see Barbara Fiand, *Embraced by Compassion: On Human Longing and Divine Response* (New York: Crossroad, 1993).

seeing, understanding, and eventually appreciating ourselves and the world.

Boelen identifies the first level of meaning as largely "bodily." It pervades our consciousness from approximately the experience of conception, life in the womb and mutual symbiosis where both mother and child benefit from their physical at-oneness, through the birth trauma of physical but not yet psychological separation, to the time of ego emergence. Here the child's experience of psychological unity with its mother, which has persisted, albeit in a lesser but nevertheless real manner after birth, is ended and the child begins to claim, and subsequently establish, his or her own identity and, therefore, separateness.

The conviction that consciousness is part of the human being from its earliest moments of life is growing in acceptance today, especially in the area of fetal psychology.[6] Researchers in psychoanalytic therapy found that one out of three persons undergoing this therapy reported that before any experience of distress and terror that can also be part of the time in the womb and certainly of the birth experience, there was a time of "sheer bliss" as early as fertilization. There seem to have been no attachments or boundaries. The experience was one of "no time, no space, no light, no dark, no right, no left, no up, no down, no masculine, no feminine—only experiential wonderment in a completely monistic state."[7] The findings of Stanislav Grof, working in this field, identify the consciousness of early prenatal existence as one of total at-onement: "It is as though I encompass the whole universe. It is I and I am it."[8] The universe here is, of course, the mother's womb. It is for the tiny life within, as I suggest below, similar to what the paleolithic tribe is for its members. It

---

[6] See Thomas Verny, MD, with John Kelly, *The Secret Life of the Unborn Child* (Ontario: Don Mills, 1981). See also Leslie Feher, *The Psychology of Birth: Roots of Human Personality* (New York: Continuum, 1981); and selected works by Stanislav Grof, especially *The Holotropic Mind: The Three Levels of Human Consciousness and How They Shape Our Lives* (San Francisco: Harper Collins, 1990), Parts I and II.

[7] June Singer, *Love's Energy* (Boston: Sigo Press, 1990), 203. Singer discusses here the findings of Stanislav Grof and Frank Lake.

[8] Singer, *Love's Energy.*

is the whole in which the blastocyst finds its existence, whereby its identity, its being, is defined, that to which it unequivocally belongs. The experience is unitive, one of total connectedness.

Grof, commenting on this "pre-personal" period of human consciousness that so clearly points to a holistic sense of oneness, sees a profoundly spiritual connection with the later experience of the transpersonal. In my past lectures on this topic I often referred to these bliss-filled moments of our beginning as periods of "unearned" mysticism—the gift of a unitive experience to which one returns much later in life and sometimes perhaps only at the moment of death.

Birth is the first existential crisis, according to Bernard Boelen. It is a major turning point for the budding human consciousness and calls for an adjustment to physical separation. The crisis can actually be quite traumatic for both mother and child because the physical intimacy is suddenly terminated and both find themselves, in a sense, isolated. A mother's "postpartum blues" can be intense, but it is the little one who especially needs affection and tenderness in order to get over the shock of physical aloneness. Boelen maintains that the nonphysical aspects of the unitive experience continue, however, to some degree for quite some time after the birth experience and are slowly severed only when the infant begins to differentiate as it focuses outward and eventually recognizes the external world as truly external and separate. The child is then impelled to identify herself or himself as different, as separate, and even "over against." The little ego begins to emerge.[9]

Level I, Paleo-Feminine Consciousness

Preamble

Beatrice Bruteau identifies the first stage of human evolutionary consciousness as paleo-*feminine*. When in my courses and work-

---

[9] For a detailed discussion on individual maturation in level one, see Boelen, *Personal Maturity,* 15–26; and also Fiand, *Embraced by Compassion,* 69–80.

shops I first presented this phenomenon of the human journey into ever wider and more profound consciousness, I frequently encountered some resistance (polite, but palpable) to the use of gender terms, and I found that an explanation was warranted before a meaningful discussion about the first stage of our cultural conscious evolution could be addressed.

Beatrice Bruteau gives this explanation early in her essay. It is clear that masculine and feminine are polar concepts that in today's research are progressively identified as complementary and present in both men and women. Unfortunately, however, viewing these polarities dualistically, denying their complementarity, is still generally prevalent in society. It has dominated our perceptions and "organized" the values and operations of our world since the beginning of the agricultural era some ten thousand years ago. Weak/strong, passive/active, submissive/dominant, feeling/thinking, emotional/intellectual, homemaker/provider are just some of the polar perceptions that still, albeit not as overtly in some parts of the world such as North America and parts of Europe, influence how we see, characterize, and then respectively ascribe the roles for women and men in our societies. The consequence of such a divide eventually can lead to oppression that often, and certainly more frequently in our time, is then met with resistance. But, as Bruteau wisely points out, the desire and attempts to turn the tables and reverse the roles does not alleviate the problem. Counter-oppression is *rebellion,* not *revolution.* It brings about no meaningful change and certainly no evolution of consciousness. Much of societal dualistic polarization with its extreme consequences is the result of isolating in women or in men the roles ascribed to each pole, that is, either to the female or the male gender. What has been discovered in recent times, however, is that the polarities cannot be separated that way. They are present in both women and men. Bruteau observes correctly:

> Sexual polarity and all its analogues . . . exist within each individual person. It is a complementary structure characterizing every man and every woman. . . . Males and

females play out *symbolically* the two aspects of being and consciousness that *actually* compose all of us.[10]

If, insisting on its symbolic nature, we then accept sexual polarity as paradigmatic for the larger social relationships that exist in human society, Bruteau suggests that *alternative* ways of experiencing it will be necessary to help bring about a new and less polarized future.

In order to facilitate this process, she points, first of all, to the basic biological femaleness of the human organism, with maleness as "a genetic and hormonal *specialization* of the general femaleness." Second, she reminds us that in the act of generation, the paternal act is one of *separation,* of "parting from." It is quick, externalizes, and *gives forth.* The mother, on the other hand, *receives into herself* and provides the place where the gametes unite, where the new life is *nurtured* and given a home for growth and development. Third, Bruteau describes "the male experience of sexual arousal and satisfaction [as] comparatively rapid, local, and *disconnected* from other aspects of life, while the female experience tends to be slow and *integral,* involving the whole body and the whole life."[11]

Bruteau sees these contrasts as suggesting an axis identifying a polarity between concepts such as (1) the specialized and the general, (2) the analytic and the synthetic, and (3) the focused and the holistic.[12] Neither pole is better than the other. Their characteristics are shared by all of us and necessary for all of us. They are complementary and, if understood and accepted that way, they help further progress and life rather than division and strife.

Level I in Ancient Times

This rather lengthy preamble was, I believe, necessary to prepare us for the period that preceded the age that we are still living

---

[10] Bruteau, *The Grand Option,* 19, italics added.
[11] Ibid., 20, italics added.
[12] Ibid., 20.

in and that Beatrice Bruteau describes as the "masculine era."
Scholars speak of the earlier period (generally identified simply
as the Paleolithic Era) as the time when Homo sapiens emerged.
Its end is estimated at between eight to ten thousand years ago,
when humans discovered agriculture. As mentioned above, Beatrice Bruteau identifies this age as paleo-*feminine*. She describes
it as marked by strong group consciousness and tribal unity,
where ostracization meant death because survival and security
were clearly connected with group protection and support. An
experience of oneness predominated, and separation seemed
intolerable, because the individual identified with the whole. For
the person there was nothing individually relevant beyond the
parameter of the group, because individuality as such was not
yet recognized. Since the themes of unity, dependence, and the
inability to survive on one's own certainly echo the consciousness
of human prenatal and neonatal existence, one could quite correctly symbolize this phase of the emergence of Homo sapiens as
the infancy phase of humankind, when what we are and continue
to become was in its embryonic, its initial stages.

For paleo-*feminine* consciousness the "outside" world was
approached communally. It was mysterious and held powers that
could not, and would not, be responded to individually, except
through the sacred practices of shamans, who were considered
gifted and called to engage these practices for the group.[13] Ani-
mism was pervasive, filling nature with life and sacred powers.
It is believed that there were widespread and generally gender-
indifferent shamanic practices of healing, and especially of contact (through altered states of consciousness) with the deceased
ancestors of the tribe in order to seek wisdom and guidance. All
of this might be considered one of the earliest forms of spirituality and manifests a deep sense of the sacred.

Bruteau's identification of this first level of consciousness as
specifically paleo-*feminine* is particularly fitting, I believe, be-

---

[13] It is estimated that shamanic practices date back between forty to
fifty thousand years. See Leo Rutherford, *Way of Shamanism* (London:
Thorsons, Harper Collins, 2001), 2.

cause the life mysteries so clearly symbolized in women's fertility and life-giving powers were a major preoccupation and concern at that time. Mother Earth was worshiped. She provided sustenance, and the hunting and gathering rights of the tribe duly paid homage to her generosity. Total dependence on her fertility marked the gathering and hunting practices of the tribe, which was compelled to move whenever the Great Mother denied sustenance in any particular place and the ancestors' guidance accordingly pointed in a different direction.

Level I, Conclusion

The first level of consciousness both in the human individual, as well as in cultural evolution, continues to be the subject of research even though it is challenging and difficult to access. One is shrouded in the mystery of womb existence, the other in ancient, pre-literate societies that have left us only hints of their affinity to later human cultures. It is my firm conviction that these explorations into the mystery of our beginning are vital since, as I mentioned already, the evolution in human personal as well as cultural consciousness is intimately connected. We deny or ignore this connection only at our own peril. The reflections dealing with the next two levels of consciousness will hopefully bring greater clarity and insight around this issue.

Level Two in Personal and Cultural Maturation

Boelen sees the second level of individual human maturation as generally "functional." This period of development can last from the time of ego emergence, roughly around the "terrible twos," through childhood and puberty, into the late teens. It is marked by a gradual unfolding of the individual *as* individual who sees the world as different from or at least for a while as even over against her or him. It progressively appears as a "differentiated and structured unity"[14] in the face of which "the budding ego

---

[14] Boelen, *Personal Maturity*, 22.

gathers itself up and takes a stand in order to identify itself to itself."[15] The initial, fundamental disposition at this time of conscious development is one of "over against-ness" and separation. It catches up to and in some way parallels on the psychic level the necessary physical separation of birth. Passivity is replaced by activity and curiosity, experimentation, questioning, and, of course, the perennial "no!" that helps reinforce the quest for independence.

It is not my intention to give a detailed description of the numerous sublevels that make up this period of maturation, interesting though they are, since the primary purpose of this essay is to explore the relationship between the personal and Beatrice Bruteau's theory of the cultural evolution of consciousness and, in this way, to highlight the responsibility that this recognition places on each one of us. Moving, then, beyond the details of the various sublevels in ego consciousness, we can simply say that over the years the young person gradually begins to claim personal power and tries to separate ever more intentionally from parental and adult control. Increasing linguistic skills, as well as the ability to differentiate and conceptualize, eventually distance the youngster from the tangible world and enhances the sense of independence. "A gradual disengagement of thought from behavioral involvement with the concrete world allows for increased ability in abstractive thinking."[16] Thus, that which is measurable, verifiable, can be controlled, and is logical increases in importance, while mystery, the unfathomable, and anything whose immediate usefulness is not clear decreases in value.

This time of maturation for the young person, even if exciting and new, can nevertheless be painful. The youngster often vehemently rejects parental guidance in favor of peer values; intentional and at times provocative behavior can make family life deeply stressful as the youngster's inner searching and confusion spills over and creates hurt and discomfort for everyone. It seems to me that this is especially true today, when much of what

---

[15] Fiand, *Embraced by Compassion*, 82.
[16] Ibid., 89.

the young person experiences is being exacerbated and exploited by a consumer society in which the gang mentality may turn out to be a much more serious problem than merely a phase in the maturation of an adolescent.

> What we refer to as "gangs" in the cities of our country today is the result, in many instances, of human developmental patterns gone awry in a society that uses the young and vulnerable for its own gain and works out its own unresolved and unacknowledged [negativity] . . . through them. Ours is an age of obsessive domination and over-againstness. It preys on healthy moments of growth, blows up the vulnerable aspects by means of advertising [and social media], and then uses every means in its power to exploit the weakest of the weak who find themselves caught there. The natural, ontological aspects of group dependency during puberty are, therefore, distorted in our time.[17]

If we now parallel even just these aspects of individual development with the emergence and development of Bruteau's "masculine era,"[18] we would have to imagine, on the cultural side, not only a gradual and similar disengagement from, but also a claim to personal power over-against the Sacred Mother, who previously provided all the necessities of life. One could picture, for example, that with an increased ability to observe and differentiate, the first humans eventually would have noticed that the seeds that certain edible plants shed onto the earth during particular seasons of the year yielded, after a period of time, identical plants in larger numbers, growing around them and adding quite naturally to the tribe's food supply. From this first observation the decision to gather up what was shed from edible plants, to sow it on cleared ground, to tend it as it sprouted, and finally to reap it, allowed the tribe to establish itself in a favorable

---

[17] Ibid., 92.
[18] Often this period of human development is referred to as the agricultural period that signaled human independence from Mother Earth.

part of its geographic location and form settlements rather than to keep roaming and foraging for food, as it had previously done. In this way a certain independence was reached where before total reliance on the great Mother had been necessary.

In a similar vein, eventual parallels could have been drawn with plant activity and human procreative acts: the shedding of seeds from man into woman during sexual union. The logical conclusion here would have been that after a period of nurture inside the woman, the seed would flourish into offspring resembling the one whose seed had been planted. A female child would, in this context, have been seen as a mistake. Aristotle's observation on the nature of woman as a "misbegotten male," that is, an error in the generative process, would have been a logical deduction in the light of the agricultural experience that was projected onto human procreation and the unique role of the sperm (seed). The ovum, and the feminine role beyond being the receptacle and nurturer of the seed, had not yet been discovered. It actually became part of human self-understanding only in 1826 through the research of Karl Ernst von Baer. The gradual movement, then, away from the Mother and everything mysterious and powerful associated with woman opened the way for what Beatrice Bruteau calls the "masculine" level of consciousness.

As we parallel, once again, the cultural and the individual levels of consciousness, Bruteau's "masculine" level of human evolution is symbolically quite readily identifiable with the adolescent age of humanity. It is easy enough to recognize in this symbolic adolescent cultural period many of the prized values of our day, even if they are broadened and intensified beyond Boelen's second level of individual maturation: for example, abstraction and objectification; the importance of self-reliance, personal ingenuity, specialization, analysis, and focus; the establishment of safe boundaries and independence; success understood as belonging to the fittest, the strongest, the most competent, those who can make it on their own; and finally, the increasing dualistic distinctions between in and out, up and down, male and female, spiritual and the material. The values Boelen sees as primary for the adolescent and late adolescent, such as competition, debate, and winning, are prized and certainly valued in the "masculine"/agricultural era of our time as well. For the adolescent the gang becomes a substitute for parental care and love, and one's own group or clique replaces all previously enjoyed relationships. For the adult in the "masculine"/agricultural era engaging the world on a climaxed "masculine" level of consciousness, the circle that controls one's values simply is wider and extends farther, in this way perpetuating the adolescent life into adulthood and perceived maturity. One's social circle, political party, religion, nationality, ethnicity, race, where one shops and eats, one's economic class, and yes, certainly still one's gender, become the isolating factors that influence today's adult's self-identification. Strength, influence, economic opportunities, and power are on the "masculine" level of consciousness identified with progress and development. What, after all, are the *developed,* the *developing*, and the *underdeveloped* countries, except constructs of artificial social and economic boundaries we have created? The tyranny of our identity circle dominates all the choices we make.

The gang that for the young person was initially simply a vehicle in the quest for separateness has in our age become the dominating criterion for adult life as well. Rules of behavior are generally functional according to economic priorities, demanding strict conformity in looks, in what car one drives, where one lives, and often even in the clothes one wears in accordance to the standards of the class to which one belongs. The class has its own rules of morality as well, obeyed unquestioningly if one wants to belong.

I feel a certain sadness as I write this. It seems that at this time in our history we are experiencing dangerous excesses of the agricultural period and its "masculine" consciousness. The violence of religious extremism, perhaps most brutally exhibited in the Middle East conflicts with Isis and its intentional exploitation and radicalization through social media of vulnerable adolescents throughout the world, is one example of the agricultural age reaching a climax that, if it remains unrecognized and therefore unchecked, can bring unprecedented suffering and destruction. Ten thousand years of dualism have created the illusion of separateness, individualism, and isolation. The excessive need for personal identity (clearly a phenomenon of Boelen's second-level consciousness) has created this illusion. We have drawn boundaries, as Ken Wilber explains, and our self-identity depends entirely on what is inside those boundaries. In Western civilization, in particular, even our body—something we "have" rather than "are"—is experienced as separate and outside our essential ego-boundary.[19] It is objectified and, on an ever-increasing scale, is becoming commercialized.

It is clear that during the "masculine"/agricultural era of consciousness pervading our culture the unitive consciousness of the paleo-*feminine* has progressively been rejected. And, whereas an initial distancing is normal and necessary for the evolution of consciousness at this level, both for the young person and within the culture as a whole, today we seem to be experiencing dangerous extremes of ego-obsession resulting in an unprecedented demonstration of "over against-ness" and consequent alienation, as well as a progressive clamor for independence and separatism.

It would, of course, be normal for us to turn to our religion for a possible solution; our faith may offer us an answer to this dilemma. The fact that most organized religions originated, however, in the last ten thousand or so years—in the agricultural era, therefore, and out of the "masculine" level of consciousness—does not offer much consolation here. Most, if not all, organized religions have masculine gods, and many, to this day, have masculine leaders (the priest, minister, bishop, pope, grand ayatollah, and so on). To this day, also, especially for the Catholic and Muslim traditions, considering a woman for a leadership role in the religious establishment is unheard of and for some even scandalous. Decisions are made for women by men. Morality is dictated on masculine terms. Even if the founders of religions saw clearly beyond gender dominance, as certainly is the case in Christianity, their teachings are still interpreted by

---

[19] Ken Wilber, *No Boundary: Eastern and Western Approaches to Personal Growth* (Boston: Shambhala Publications, 1979), 4–7.

today's leaders within the "masculine" level of consciousness: logically, legalistically, dualistically, exclusivist, and predominantly content rather than praxis oriented. Their leadership and world perspective beyond the functional, "masculine" vision is, therefore, difficult to fathom.

For the adolescent the functional level reaches a pivotal point during puberty—a period of chaos and confusion caused largely by the intense conflict the young person experiences between what Boelen identifies as the "body-subject" and the "body-object," that is, the ego and "its" body. The latter is in complete chaos and cannot be controlled any longer by the ego. "In the extremity of conflict created in the youngster's own ontological dilemma, however, the stage is set for yet another turning point and breakthrough into deeper openness."[20] Boelen calls this period of crisis the "negative phase of adolescence" and reassures the reader that eventually the spiral turns. First, however, there is much internal struggle, expressed outwardly through what might best be described as intentional "ugliness" often physically inflicted by the youngster on her or his own body (spiked hair, tattoos, nose rings, and so forth) and further demonstrated by creating a cluttered and messy personal environment. Socially ugly and rude behavior is also expressed toward family, teachers, and the adult world as a whole.

This deeply unpleasant period of development is finally followed by a time of often intense frustration, "lost-ness," and helplessness during which the young person slowly begins to realize that her or his perceived reality is no longer sufficient or able to answer his or her emerging and urgent inner questions. A growing loss of confidence in the abstract and functional world in which the youngster has felt at home for quite some time and an increased disenchantment with the institutions rightly or wrongly associated with it make life a wasteland with nowhere to turn.

The reason for this, quite simply, is that the "personal" level of openness (Level Three) has not yet *dawned* for him or

---

[20] Fiand, *Embraced by Compassion*, 93.

her. Since adult institutions carry significance in accordance with the youngster's level of awareness, they are generally seen within the levels of functionality [that have not as yet been transcended]. It stands to reason that when these are resented, so is anything viewed by their standards. . . . As these are the only ones the young person knows, *at this time*, a whole-scale of rejection of life in general [including religion and morality] is not uncommon.[21]

From a symbolic perspective it is interesting to note here the parallels, once again, between the struggling youngster in the maturation process and the social crisis of today as our culture is suffering through the end, but also the climax, of the "masculine"/ agricultural era—its *cultural adolescence*. Many of us today are experiencing a general disenchantment with many of the institutions we have grown up with and in, and were taught to respect. A growing lack of trust in our political structures and in government in general is also evident. Many of us seem to be moving beyond many of the declarations made by our religious leaders and, on occasion, openly distancing ourselves from them. There is, for some, a puzzling tolerance with modern culture, with behaviors and lifestyles that were feared and even condemned in the past. At the same time there is evidence also of genuine dismay, voiced openly and frequently, with much of the random violence, dishonesty, and lack of mutual respect everywhere in the world. "What, on earth, is happening today?" we ask. Or, "How can this be happening in our country? Where did all this violence, aggression, hatred, sexual promiscuity, unnecessary greed, and competition come from?" We want someone to "fix it," but we have lost faith in most of our elected representatives as well as ecclesial leadership.

Although materialism has certainly not been abandoned by Western society as a whole and seems in fact to be at an all time high, we are beginning to hear and to see with dismay what it is doing to hundreds and thousands of people who are

---

[21] Ibid., 95.

near starvation; to refugees; to those who are being trafficked for economic gain, promiscuous satisfaction, and even body parts. Slavery is widespread, not only in faraway places, but in our very affluent Western countries as well. Pollution is wreaking havoc with our environment, endangering not only our lives, but also those of all our fellow creatures on this globe. Violence is reported daily on the news, and war seems to be the only way we are attempting to "fix" the world's terrifying dilemma. The one-sidedness of a "masculine"/agrarian culture with its major emphasis on the material values is becoming evident, and a genuine revolution of consciousness appears to be desperately needed.

Level Three in Personal and Cultural Maturation

Regarding the adolescent at the end of puberty, Boelen reassures us that the painful experiences of this time in the youngster's life hold within them a depth dimension that ultimately emerges and, when it does, challenges the young person to look beyond the "thingness of things," beyond their apparent value and usefulness, as it were, and to allow for a movement toward an unexpected, direct, and unequivocal encounter with the no-*thingness* of all things.

> The pain of this can be excruciating, since the youngster experiences in all its intensity the hollowing out that is necessary for him or her ultimately to embrace his or her personhood in the empty, open receptivity and response-ability that it is.[22]

And it is this "hollowing out" that prepares the way for the third level of consciousness that Bernard Boelen identifies as the level of personal maturity. It seems almost counterintuitive (for the parent, I suspect, it seems more like a miracle), but the painful experience eventually does give way to a deeper appreciation of life and of human interaction in general. The young person,

---

[22] Ibid.

often quite suddenly and unexpectedly, opens up to wonder and beauty and, with that, there begins the actual movement into the authentic self.

Beatrice Bruteau refers to the cultural equivalent of Boelen's personal maturity (that has, in fact, not arrived yet and can only be surmised) as "neo-feminine." She makes it clear that because

> the coming revolution in consciousness is truly new, a genuine radical shift in our basic perceptions, we cannot possibly know what form it will take. But because it will be another turn on the evolutionary spiral, we may project that it will bear some basic resemblance to its counterparts on earlier levels, as well as distinguish itself by a striking difference from the most recent period [the masculine era]. Nevertheless, it will assume and incorporate all preceding stages, preserving and utilizing their advantageous qualities.[23]

Fortunately, anthropological explorations into human consciousness at the earliest stages of cultural development (Bruteau's paleo-*feminine* age) and studies of the neonate's and possibly the embryo's "openness to meaning," described by Bernard Boelen and also Stanislav Grof, offer us some interesting insights that help us surmise what the next level of consciousness might look like. Furthermore, scientific research into the nature of reality at the atomic and subatomic levels, as well as into our universe and beyond, have vastly expanded our sense of who we are as part of this world and of our human possibilities.

The discovery of universal interconnectedness seriously challenged the dualism on which the agrarian/"masculine" culture was built. This challenge, originating in its own discipline, was not welcomed with great enthusiasm by the scientific academy of the early twentieth century, steeped as it was in Newtonian principles that belonged unquestioningly to the agrarian/"masculine" era. Although firmly rooted in and indebted to the methods of

---

[23] Bruteau, *The Grand Option*, 18.

scientific observation and research birthed in that period of human development, the great physicists of the early twentieth century nevertheless moved courageously beyond the initial shock (caused at times by their own discoveries) and, even without the support of their academy, surrendered to the new. Early twentieth century research revealed that, as Danah Zohar (physicist, psychologist, and philosopher) puts it: "Things and events once conceived as separate, parted in both space and time, are seen by the quantum theorist so integrally linked that their bond mocks the reality of both space and time. They behave, instead, as multiple aspects of some larger whole."[24] Zohar moves even beyond this insight and broadens it to include all of us in a vision of unity and interconnectedness:

> In a quantum psychology, there are no isolated persons. Individuals do exist, do have an identity, a meaning and a purpose; but, like particles, each of them is a brief manifestation of a particularity. This particularity is in nonlocal correlation with all other particularities and to some extent interwoven with them. Everything that each of us does affects all the rest of us, directly and physically. I am my brother's keeper because he is a part of me, just as my hand is a part of my body. If I injure my hand, my whole body hurts. If I injure my consciousness—fill it with malicious or evil or selfish thoughts—I injure the whole nonlocally connected "field" of consciousness. Each of us, because of [our] integral relationship with others, with Nature, and with the whole world of values, has the capacity to beatify or to taint the waters of eternity. Each of us therefore carries, as a result of [our] quantum nature, an awesome moral responsibility. I am responsible for the world because, in the words of the late Krishnamurti, "I am the world."[25]

---

[24] Danah Zohar, *The Quantum Self: Human Nature and Consciousness Defined by the New Physics* (New York: Quill/William Morrow, 1990), 34.

[25] Zohar, *The Quantum Self*, 169, 170.

Psychologist Carl Jung speaks similarly when he points out that "if things go wrong in the world, this is because something is wrong with the individual, because something is wrong with me. Therefore, if I am sensible, I shall put myself right first."[26] It is claimed that Buddhist Zen master Thich Nhat Hanh, when asked who had caused the war in Iraq, responded without hesitation: "I did." Universal interconnectedness, being to being, each of us to, in, and through everything else! The discoveries in this regard throughout the twentieth and now in the twenty-first century are astounding:

- Einstein's widely known discovery of an omnicentric universe, putting each of us and every other reality in the universe at the center of its expansion;[27]
- the discovery of quantum reality's "response" to the intention of the researcher studying it, having, therefore, some form of "relationality";[28]
- Hal Puthoff and Russel Targ's experiments with altered states of consciousness enabling "long-distance viewing" (a nonphysical transcendence of space and even of time) recorded for the CIA;[29]
- Elizabeth Targ's well-documented clinical experiment with the long-distance healing of end-stage AIDS patients;[30]
- Cleve Backster's experiments with plant and animal consciousness, intelligence, empathy, and memory, which he called "primary perception."[31]

---

[26] Jung, quoted in Zohar, *The Quantum Self*, 170.

[27] For a discussion of this, see Brian Swimme, *The Hidden Heart of the Cosmos, Humanity and the New Story* (Maryknoll, NY: Orbis Books, 1996), 71–73.

[28] Lynne McTaggart, *The Field: The Quest for the Secret Force of the Universe* (New York: Harper Collins, 2002), 11.

[29] Ibid., chap. 8.

[30] Ibid., 181–89.

[31] Marilyn Ferguson, *The Brain Revolution: The Frontiers of Mind Research* (New York: Bantam Books, 1975), 351. See also Franci Prowse, with Cleve Baxter, "Exploring a Sentient World," *Shift: At the Frontiers of Consciousness,* no. 11 (June-August 2006): 20–23.

These, and so many more, all invite us to reevaluate and to let go of our propensity to understand ourselves and our reality as disconnected, distinct, isolated, independent from, and often even superior to, everything else. We are discovering today, through numerous experiments and experiences, that we are part of the whole and that, paradoxically but also holographically, the whole is also inside each of us. Ken Wilber sees the consciousness that invites us beyond the artificial boundaries we have created to establish our identity and separateness as "transpersonal." It implies "an expansion of the self/not-self boundary."[32]

Once again, Danah Zohar writes eloquently about the shift in our self-identity that is required of us as we ponder the discoveries of science that are heralding for us a completely new way of understanding ourselves and inviting us to a new level in consciousness:

> With a quantum view of process, it becomes clear in a new way that "I," not just my atoms or my genes, but my personal being—the pattern that is me—will be part and parcel of all that is to come, just as it is part of the nexus of now and, indeed, was in large part foreshadowed in the past. . . . There is no real division in space or time between selves. We are all individuals, but individuals within a greater unity, a unity that defines each of us in terms of others and gives each of us a stake in eternity. . . . We know that quantum physics calls upon us to alter our notions of space and time, but now we have to accept that this touches each and every one of us at the core of our personhood.[33]

That these insights are emerging from a discipline that finds its origin and pride of place on the "masculine"/agricultural level of consciousness could seem ironic were it not for Bernard Boelen's observation that the suffering and disenchantment of late

---

[32] Wilber, *No Boundary,* 8.
[33] Zohar, *The Quantum Self,* 151.

adolescence and, for that matter, of any subsequent existential crisis bears within itself the seeds of what is yet to come. Surely the violent excesses of the "masculine"/agricultural era that we are experiencing at this time in history have us concerned and yearning for a better, more noble, humble, honest dimension of our common humanity. But *our yearning is in fact already the seed of its emergence.*

One can feel relief, as it were, when one studies the quantum view of reality and learns that somehow humanity is part of this extraordinary phenomenon, not separate from it. It makes me turn to the great visionaries of our time and appreciate once more their wisdom. Perhaps the compassion for the poor and oppressed and the down-to-earth humanness of Pope Francis have such popular appeal at the moment, not just for Catholics but for people throughout the world, because he touches *what is emerging in human consciousness as a whole* and verifies our fundamental "at-oneness." He experiences life with the "participatory consciousness" that Beatrice Bruteau identifies in her remarks on the neo-feminine:

> When I love with participatory consciousness, I see that what the other *is* is some of my life-energy living there, and what I *am,* is some of the other's life-energy living here in me. I can no longer divide the world into "we's" and "they's." I have an awareness of one large life circulating through all. In some way, my boundary has become less definite, in the sense of being less hard and sealed off. My selfhood has become radiant, streaming out from me, and is found participating in the other even as it is found in me. . . . The single large life in which I participate is a community of whole unique selves who freely form and constitute this large unifying life by the intercommunication of their creative love energies.[34]

Bruteau sees participatory consciousness as primarily lived and modeled by Jesus. The energy that ultimately empowers the

---

[34] Bruteau, *The Grand Option*, 29–30.

neo-*feminine* is love that affirms the goodness of what is *as* it is and in this way empowers. It is "an outflow of positive energy intending that life should become more abundant. It is *creative* love, in which one gives of one's own life to foster the life in others."[35] No wonder Teilhard de Chardin saw our discovery of and living in this kind of love as akin to discovering fire. It springs, as Bruteau insists, from our very existence as being to-gether with others in this world; an "I" exuding sheer life-energy, reaching out to others as "radiant life-energy centers" as well. I cannot help thinking (along with Beatrice Bruteau[36]) of Paul's insistence: I live, yet not I, but Christ lives in me (Gal 2:20). Teihlard's Cosmic Christ, who calls us beyond the functional, beyond definitions, "essence categories," and declarations of certitude, into the living presence of love, into life lived with a true *sense* of the other: "because I live, you are living also."[37] The love of participatory consciousness is not primarily emotional or instinctual; neither is it purely rational or abstract. Having gone through the previous levels in consciousness and having appropriated the positive aspects of each, "it grasps what it understands as a whole, as a real concrete being, as a unique instance or self, not as a member of a class or in terms of its categorizable attributes."[38] Knowing and encountering others in this way is for Bruteau "an act of spiritual sympathy" that is centered in its own active subjectivity and meets the other there.

Bernard Boelen's personal maturity understood in the con-text of Bruteau's participatory consciousness will have had to pass through young adulthood, will have needed yet another existential crisis or turning point, which he calls the "crisis of the limits," and will have entered the "second half of life," or what Carl Jung calls "individuation." During this journey into maturation much of what Bruteau's "masculine" consciousness holds dear will have been called into question. The person, once again, will have seen her or his "world" fall apart. Many of the

---

[35] Ibid., 29.
[36] Ibid., 31.
[37] Ibid., 30.
[38] Ibid., 31.

choices made during one's adult life are questioned during this period and rethought. Shipwrecks of former careers and commitments can happen. The hollowing out experienced earlier returns, but now at a much deeper level. The crisis of individuation calls for a radical reevaluation of all values. The insights that emerge during this time come mostly through suffering:

> One learns to let-be, to hold oneself in one's poverty. One learns that poverty is blessed; that the hungry will be filled; that one is loved because one *is,* not because one *does.* One learns about the brotherhood and sisterhood of the human family; about the responsibility that truly loving another calls forth, the freedom and empowerment it entails. One learns of the commonality of sin and of redemption that was always there, waiting, and never needed to be earned or "lived up to." One heals even as one recognizes the "sting in the flesh," and in the healing one becomes whole.[39]

Authentic maturation, occurring primarily in the second half of life, is the journey from "ego" values and boundaries, from Beatrice Bruteau's "masculine" consciousness, into the *self.* It is the challenge of authentic human existence. In the words of T. S. Eliot, it is "a condition of complete simplicity / (Costing not less than everything)."[40]

Our Existential Challenge

Bruteau ends her reflection on neo-*feminine* consciousness by asking whether it is actually possible for us "to enter into such a transformed state of consciousness" and truly to evolve; that is, whether populations and cultures can do this. She firmly believes that it *can* happen because some have succeeded in this

---

[39] Fiand, *Embraced by Compassion,* 105.
[40] T. S. Eliot, "Little Gidding V," *Four Quartets* (1943).

process, "have been born again." After ten thousand years or more of "masculine"/agricultural consciousness, the temptation, of course, is to believe that things are as they have always been and that what has always been cannot change. But this attitude forgets that there have also always been the exceptions, the great visionaries and ethical geniuses that have pointed beyond the here and now to what can be and is already present in all of us. Some have suffered for their convictions and died, but because of our inherent drive toward greater complexity or beauty and wholeness, or as Teilhard de Chardin would say, toward authentic "co-being" or love, their vision eventually began to challenge us, take root, and was vindicated. Our culture has to count on this, as each of us, over and over again by our efforts and actions for the sake of humanity, and unquestionably through grace, adds to the critical mass[41] and "leans into" the turning of the evolutionary spiral.

I firmly believe that we all, as part of the whole and in "a condition of complete simplicity / costing no less than everything," are responsible for the whole. Our behavior has consequences, and as we mature and become part of the revolution in consciousness, our culture as a whole will benefit. The juxtaposition of Bernard Boelen's philosophy of individual maturation and Beatrice Bruteau's vision of the cultural evolution in consciousness has hopefully demonstrated that there is a *common human destiny* that holds the *one* inextricably linked to the *many*. Cultures are composed of individuals. Each of us is accountable. "We ourselves *are* the future," Beatrice Bruteau once again reminds us, "and we *are* the revolution."[42]

> *Creator of every kind of paradox and puzzle,*
> *Evolutionary Spirit,*

---

[41] Based on the theory that if enough members of a species (some estimate it to be a mere 1 percent) change behavior, the entire species will ultimately do so.

[42] Bruteau, *The Grand Option*, 32.

Persuade us to learn wisdom
from the alive and eloquent universe.
You are our God, the God with us and beyond us.
We hope to be your joy.[43]

---

[43] William Cleary, *Prayers to an Evolutionary God* (Woodstock, VT: Skylight Paths Publishing, 2004), 54. Excerpts from the prayer "Your Joy—When Pursuing Wisdom."

4

Teilhard, the Trinity, and Evolution

The Journey Continues

CYNTHIA BOURGEAULT

When anything really new begins to germinate around us, we cannot distinguish it—for the very good reason that it could only be recognized in the light of what it is going to be.

—PIERRE TEILHARD DE CHARDIN,
The Human Phenomenon

It has often been noted that in his sweeping new vision of Christian metaphysics Teilhard makes curiously little use of the Trinity. While one can hardly second guess a mystic his sources of inspiration, clearly a significant contributing factor was that the Trinity he knew from the Scholastic theology of his times left him little to work with. Never much of a fan of Scholasticism anyway, Teilhard seemed to find trinitarian systematics particularly off-putting, describing the presentation as "over-intricate, outlandish, and superfluous."[1] He doubted that it would have much to offer the modern mind.

In retrospect, this appears to be one of those great missed opportunities, for had he been able to see the Trinity from the perspective of our own theological times, I believe he would have been quick to recognize a congenial terrain and a rich new vein of inspiration for his theological imagination. My essay is offered as a first attempt to bring the Teilhardian canon into direct dialogue with the emerging vision of the Trinity that has taken shape in the half-century following his death, either directly or indirectly under his influence. In the first part of my study I introduce the major players in this conversation and highlight their individual contributions, taking particular note of the pivotal contribution made by Beatrice Bruteau. In the second part I explore what happens when we attempt to transpose Teilhard's magnificent intellectual edifice onto this new trinitarian foundation. As I hope to demonstrate, not only do the two complement and contextualize each other, but in the process they allow us to glimpse a whole new "ternary" way of doing metaphysics that might well prove to be Christianity's most significant contribution to the ongoing evolutionary dialogue.

A New Breed of Trinity

Catherine LaCugna

The trinitarian renaissance of our times was stirred into action in 1967, when Teilhard's younger Jesuit colleague Karl Rahner issued his terminal prognosis that the Trinity had become so irrelevant to the actual practice of Christianity that "should the doctrine of the Trinity have to be dropped as false, the major part of religious literature could well remain virtually unchanged."[2] But it would take another two decades before

---

[1] Pierre Teilhard de Chardin, *Christianity and Evolution,* trans. Bernard Wall (New York: Harcourt Brace, 1974), 157.

[2] Karl Rahner, *The Trinity* (New York: Crossroad, 2013; 1st ed. 1970), ix.

Catherine Mowry LaCugna, following in his footsteps, succeeded in rescuing the Trinity from the theological margins to which it had increasingly been relegated, restoring it to active duty as a foundational symbol of Christian life. Her 1991 book *God for Us: The Trinity and Christian life,* marked a tipping point in trinitarian studies, not only because of the rigor of her scholarship and passion of her argument, but because its publication by the prestigious popular press HarperSanFrancisco succeeded at last in putting the Trinity on the public radar screen.

In the first part of her book LaCugna traces what she calls the "defeat" of the doctrine of the Trinity over a thousand years of development, as it moved from an original participative vision of God's redemptive work in the world to an increasingly abstract speculation on the inner life of God. Once that fundamental rupture had occurred between God *in se* ("in himself"; the immanent or theological Trinity) and God *pro nobis* ("for us"; the economic Trinity), the drift continued to widen—in the Christian East through an exaggerated differentiation between the "essence" and "energies" of God, and in the post-Augustinian West through an increasing fixation on the substance and psychology of the divine Persons. More and more the Trinity came to be locked up in a speculative realm all its own, with no connection to either the physical reality of the cosmos or the practical and moral reality of Christian life.

"The 'economic' Trinity *is* the 'immanent' Trinity" had been Rahner's celebrated clarion call.[3] LaCugna's work both nuances that assessment and develops it still further. As she sees it, "There is neither an economic nor an immanent Trinity; there is only the *Oikonomia* that is the concrete realization of the mystery of *theologia* in time, space, history, and personality. In this framework the doctrine of the Trinity encompasses more than the immanent Trinity envisioned in static ahistorical and transeconomic terms; the subject matter of the Christian theology of God is one dynamic movement of God, *a Patre ad Patrem.*"[4]

---

[3] Ibid., 22.

[4] Catherine Mowry LaCugna, *God for Us: The Trinity and Christian Life* (San Francisco: HarperSanFrancisco, 1991), 222.

While LaCugna makes no direct mention of Teilhard in her work, it is clear that her vision of the *Oikonomia* as a parabolic curve sweeping in one unbroken motion from Alpha to Omega certainly creates a stage on which Teilhard's evolutionary vision can play beautifully. Both dynamism and directionality are well represented, as well as that fundamental Teilhardian leitmotif that there is, indeed, a "comprehensive plan of God reaching creation to consummation"[5] *"in quo omnia constant* [in which all things hold together]."

Raimon Panikkar

Raimon Panikkar worked on the Trinity for most of his long and productive scholarly career, and in the nearly forty years that lie between his early *The Trinity and the Religious Experience of Man* (1973) and his final magnum opus, *The Rhythm of Being* (2010), we watch him moving incrementally toward an understanding of the Trinity as an all-encompassing ground of being—essentially, a dead ringer for Teilhard's "divine milieu." By his 2004 work, *Christophany,* he is characterizing the Trinity as "pure relationality"; "the dynamism of the real."[6] His final pronouncement on the subject is a jaw-dropping one-liner that in itself could easily furnish the agenda for the entire next generation of Christian evolutionary research: "By Trinity, I mean the ultimate triadic structure of reality."[7]

Panikkar's extensive body of work is complementary in many respects to Teilhard's, although he seems to make very little actual use of Teilhard in the development of his own thought. Both are concerned to open up a Christian self-understanding that has become an *amor curvus*, as Panikkar calls it, a closed circle, to receive new inputs from a world rapidly outpacing it in both coherence and scope. If Teilhard's primary conversation is with

---

[5] LaCugna, *God for Us*, 223.

[6] Raimon Panikkar, *Christophany* (Maryknoll, NY: Orbis Books, 2004), 103, xx.

[7] Raimon Panikkar, *The Rhythm of Being: The Guifford Lectures* (Maryknoll, NY: Orbis Books, 2010), 55.

science, Panikkar, that great interspiritual pioneer, is primarily in conversation with the great spiritual traditions of the world, particularly the *advaita* of the East. While their methods and audiences differ, the same fundamental conviction drives them; that is, that if Christianity is, as it claims, a universal vision, it must make itself universally intelligible.

Both Teilhard and Panikkar chafed against the traditional Judeo-Christian monotheism, its foundations resting squarely on an ontological dichotomy between spirit and matter and a Creator who does not personally indwell his creation. These antiquated metaphysical givens are simply no longer intellectually sustainable in a world now resting firmly on an Einsteinian foundation, where energy rather than *substantia* is the coin of the realm. While Teilhard perhaps injudiciously used the word *pantheism* to convey his holographic intuition of the divine Whole permeating all of its parts, Panikkar's equivalent term covers most of these same bases while sidestepping most of its more obvious difficulties.

Cosmotheandric is Panikkar's neologism of choice to describe the trinitarian dynamism at the heart of the divine relational ground. The word is a fusion of *cosmos* (world), *theos* (God), and *andros* (man) and suggests a continuous intercirculation among these three distinct planes of existence in a single motion of self-communicating love. The gist of this idea has already been brilliantly portended in those profound images that cascade from Jesus's mouth in the farewell discourse of John 13—17: "I am the vine, you are the branches; abide in me as I in you" (John 15:4); "As you, Father, are in me and I am in you, may they may be completely one" (John 17:21–23). The vision is of a dynamic, interabiding oneness whose "substance" is inseparable from the motion itself. For Panikkar, this is Trinity, understood as a primordial metaphysical principle. It is a world of dynamic interabiding in which both unity and particularity are preserved by adding as the third term between them the dynamism itself. *Advaita* in motion, one might call it.

In fact, one of Panikkar's most profound contributions to the present trinitarian renaissance may well be his closely argued demonstration in *Christophany* that the Trinity is indeed an "original" component of Christianity—because it originates in the mind of Christ! While the fully articulated doctrine of the Trinity came into existence only in the fourth century, Panikkar argues that its real roots lie in the lived reality of Jesus's own relationship with God. It portrays that reality together in a way that is faithful to the experience itself and projects it outward as an access route through which others can enter. Between the poles of maximum unity (conveyed in Jesus's powerful assertion, "The Father and I are one") and maximum differentiation (conveyed in his shockingly tender "*Abba*, Father") flows an unbroken current of kenotic love (representing spirit) through which all things are invited to participate in that one great cosmotheandric intercirculation. For Panikkar, the Trinity is not a theological add-on; it is a manifesting principle of the first order, linking the visible and invisible realms together according to a single relational dynamism that he summarizes as follows: "I am one with the source insofar as I too act as a source by making everything I have received flow again—just like Jesus."[8]

Beatrice Bruteau

When it comes to connecting the dots between the Trinity and evolution, no one has done it more thoroughly than Beatrice Bruteau. In her 1997 book, *God's Ecstasy: The Creation of a Self-Creating World,* she explicitly identifies the Trinity as a cosmogonic principle, in fact, *the* cosmogonic principle. And with an academic background whose wingspan rivals Teilhard's (advanced degrees in both philosophy and mathematics), she is able to bring her considerable scientific and philosophical acumen to bear as she lays out exactly how and why the Trinity is all about evolution.

For Bruteau, the Trinity is first and foremost an image of symbiotic unity—in fact, it is "the original symbiotic unity." The three "God-persons in community," as she sees it, comprise

---

[8] Panikkar, *Christophany,* 116.

the prototype and the *prerequisite* for the expression of agape love, the constituent energy of the Godhead itself. In chapter 2 she builds a detailed philosophical case for why threefoldness is the necessary precondition for agape love. She then goes on to demonstrate why threefoldness is by nature "ecstatic" or, in other words, self-projective. By its very threefoldness it "breaks symmetry" (a term felicitously borrowed from the world of quantum mechanics) and projects the agape loves outward, calling new forms of being into existence, each of which bears the imprint of the original symbiotic unity that created it. With that initial premise established, her book then leads the reader through a magnificent overview of evolution, phylum by phylum, as we see the actual mechanics of the "complexification" intuited by Teilhard being played out all under the sway of this dynamic ordering principle. "It is the presence of the Trinity as a pattern repeated at every scale of the cosmic order," she believes, "that makes the universe a manifestation of God and itself sacred and holy."[9]

Bruteau is arguably Teilhard's most brilliant student, and her work moves his own a significant step forward. Her Trinity, revisioned as an evolutionary template, furnishes the mechanics to fulfill the major stipulations of Teilhard's visionary mysticism. In particular, she is able to put chapter and verse under his intuition of a dynamism, a direction, and an intrinsic ordering principle, calling all things to "Be more, Be in every possible way, Communicate Being, and Be a new whole by interaction" (her pithy summation of the Teilhardian "zest for living").[10] From a standpoint of a half-century, farther along in the pertinent scientific fields, particularly astrophysics and cellular biology, she is also able to confirm and update his basic presentation made so brilliantly in *The Phenomenon of Man*.

But while she is overwhelmingly onboard with the Teilhard program (she is, after all, one of the original founders of the

---

[9] Beatrice Bruteau, *God's Ecstasy: The Creation of a Self-Creating World* (New York: Crossroad, 1997), 14.

[10] Bruteau, *God's Ecstasy*, 58.

Teilhard Society!), this does not equate to a blind loyalty incapable of recognizing some of its significant shortcomings. One of these, for certain, is a curiously xenophobic Catholicism that leaves him unable to appreciate the potential contributions of other religious traditions, particularly those of the East. "We must note with sadness," she writes, "that it is one of the ironies of his brilliant career that Teilhard, whose doctrines of cosmic divinity and evolving consciousness so resemble certain strains of Hindu thought, had a very slight knowledge of this tradition and even less respect for it."[11] From her own extensive background in Vedanta she is able to mount a considerably more nuanced discussion of consciousness than Teilhard's, which in turn leads her to a significantly different conclusion about the ultimate outcome of the evolutionary process.

Approached from the contemporary perspective of levels of consciousness as developed in the work of Ken Wilber and others,[12] it becomes quickly apparent that Teilhard has basically no concept of what would now be called the third tier or nondual states of awareness. His notion of consciousness, founded squarely in Cartesian rationalism, is entirely centered in the *self-reflective* property of consciousness—the capacity to stand outside itself and mirror itself back ("bend back upon itself," in Teilhard's language), so as to become aware of its own awareness. For Teilhard, this self-reflective capacity is the extraordinary human breakthrough that launches the noosphere and inaugurates a whole new rung on the evolutionary ladder. But apparently unperceived by Teilhard, self-reflexive awareness can unfold in two different ways: either by *representing* itself to itself, as if in third person, or by an immediate, holographic perception of its

---

[11] Beatrice Bruteau, *Evolution toward Divinity* (Wheaton, IL: The Theosophical Publishing House, 1974), 2.

[12] See in particular Ken Wilber, *Integral Spirituality* (Boston: Shambhala Publications, 2006). The diagram of the levels of consciousness is on an overleaf, opposite page 68. Another popular and influential map is the Spiral Dynamics model developed by Don Beck (Christopher C. Cowan and Don Edward Beck, *Spiral Dynamics* [Malden, MA: Blackwell Publishing, 2013; 1st ed. 1996]).

own subjectivity. This latter mode of perception, characterized by the collapse of the subject/object pole that establishes the field of perception at the lower levels of consciousness, is what is meant by non-dual awareness, and in the Eastern traditions (and much of Western mysticism as well) it comprises a much more subtle level of conscious attainment. Teilhard's inability to spot it identifies his thinking as operating exclusively within the limits of the "higher rational" bandwidths of consciousness ("pluralistic" and "integral," in Wilber's terminology); he is certainly well ahead of the curve in his own times—and even in our own—but arguably a notch below the level needed to match the mystical unity he is intuiting. From this "level confusion" in his thinking enter two of the most controversial elements in his teaching: his understanding of personhood as "super-centration," and his insistence upon an ultimate point of convergence. Bruteau's non-dual exegesis of Teilhard's work in these respects may in the long run prove to be her greatest gift to him, creating an access route for those who applaud his vision but lament his interspiritual insensitivity and apparent inability to escape the gravitational field of traditional Western rationalism.

In her penultimate chapter in *God's Ecstasy*, entitled "The Self-Creating Universe: Pathway to Consciousness," Bruteau clarifies the distinction between these two modes of perception. In contrast to the dualistic levels of consciousness, which tend to establish identity through its *descriptions* (the set of characteristics that define it by differentiating it from others in that same category), non-dual consciousness—or "mystical," as she calls it here,

> is the immediacy and irreducibility of a subjective experience of knowing by *being* instead of by *representing*. The object of consciousness is in this case the subject itself. When the subject is aware of the subject, not by reflection—that is, not by making a representation of the subject or the act of being conscious or the concept of "being the knower—but the subject is aware of the subject by being aware *as* subject—aware as subject of subject by *being*

subject, in a fully luminous (not unaware or unconscious) way, that consciousness is "mystical."[13]

Through the lens of this luminous perception she is able to come to an understanding very different from Teilhard's of what constitutes a person:

Usually we think of this "I" in terms of our descriptions: gender, race, age, relationships, work, history, personality type, cultural commitments, and so on. These give us a feeling of definiteness (which we confuse with reality) by defining how we are different from others. I am I by being not-you. I have a different description. . . . All those categories of descriptions may be said to characterize our "nature" as distinct from ourselves as "persons." The natures are different from each other by "mutual negation." What one has another does not; it has something the first does not. This is how their definitions are made. But persons are not defined. So persons are not "different" from one another. Persons are absolutely unique; they are not identified by reference to one another, not compared with others, even to say they are "different." But this does not mean they all collapse into some undifferentiated union with each other and can't be "told apart." Persons are different, but it's by another kind of differentiation, not mutual negation.[14]

What is this "other kind of differentiation"? Bruteau's unitive insight here, drawn not from speculation but from the direct practice of meditation, marks the radical fork in the road between Teilhard's evolutionary assessment and her own:

Persons are beings, and being is self-diffusive, active, and self-communicating. When we ourselves, in meditation, strip away all the descriptions and center in our bare I AM,

---

[13] Bruteau, *God's Ecstasy,* 162.
[14] Ibid., 27–28.

we discover it is a radiant energy, it goes out from itself. The same reality, the same act of be-ing that says I AM enstatically, in the same breath pronounces the ecstatic MAY YOU BE. This is how Being is, and person is fundamental Being. The act of being "I is not an act of negating another, but of affirming another."[15]

The immediate implication of this, in terms of Teilhardian metaphysics, is that ultimate personhood (Teilhard's "superhuman" and "hyper-personalized") is established not by *centration*—increasing differentiation—but by what we would today term *interbeing,* the capacity to mutually interpenetrate and form new evolutionary units. "What if true persons are circles whose centers are nowhere and whose circumferences are everywhere?" she ponders in her essay "Prayer and Identity"[16]—a thought that would no doubt have left Teilhard scratching his head. And on the basis of this, two deductions follow that represent a radical departure from his own mystical scenario:

1. God must exist as a "community of God-persons" to express this radically diffusive and interabiding nature of love. The Omega Point, if such there be, cannot be identified with a single person of the Trinity but is expressed in the symbiotic unity of the whole.

2. Because of the inherent nature of Being to "Be more, Be in every possible way, Communicate Being, and Be a new whole by interaction,"[17] the more likely the evolutionary trajectory does not entail an Omega Point but a continuing open-ended expansion.

Wherever one's personal preferences may lie on this issue, it is certainly good to have options so that the validity of Teilhard's

---

[15] Ibid., 28.

[16] Beatrice Bruteau, "Prayer and Identity" (1983), in Thomas Keating et al., *Spirituality, Contemplation, and Transformation: Writings on Centering Prayer* (New York: Lantern Books, 2008), 110.

[17] Bruteau, *God's Ecstasy*, 58.

entire evolutionary vision does not rest on his ultimately personal mystical intuition of a final convergence in Christ. While I tend toward that resolution myself (on the basis of my work with the Law of Three, shortly to be introduced), Bruteau's exegesis of the Trinity on the basis of "the expansive, or radiant, character of Being"[18] is a brilliant bridge builder, not only with the non-dual metaphysical traditions, but with contemporary science as well. In particular, her recognition of threeness as "symmetry breaking"[19] and hence implicitly involved in all ongoing dynamism, brilliantly links the Trinity to evolution by logical necessity, not simply theological stipulation. At the same time it confirms that the early church's intuitive gravitation toward a model of threeness as represented in those "God-persons in community" may not be nearly so arbitrary as naysayers over the ages have claimed, but rather finds its rationale in a deeper causal ground.

The Holy Trinity and the Law of Three

My own contribution to this ongoing trinitarian conversation takes up at exactly the point that Bruteau's leaves off. Her notion of a necessary threefoldness as the driveshaft of evolution moves our understanding of the Trinity as a cosomogonic template to a whole new level. My goal has been to see whether it might be possible to anchor this necessary threefoldness not in a hypothetical three God-persons in community (which is still a theological stipulation and as such inaccessible as a starting point to all those not already so convinced) but in a deeper universal principle that I had become familiar with through my ten years of participation in Gurdjieff's Work as the Law of Three.

G. I. Gurdjieff (1866–1949) is not a name widely known in theological circles, so a few words of introduction are probably in order. This Armenian-born spiritual teacher became convinced in his early adulthood that there still existed ancient wisdom schools preserving cosmic knowledge that had long been lost to

---

[18] Ibid., 24.
[19] Ibid., 84.

contemporary humankind. After a twenty-year search, mostly in Central Asia (he and Teilhard were crisscrossing much of the same terrain a few decades apart), he arrived back in Russia on the eve of World War I and began sharing the fruits of his research. Displaced steadily westward by the political turmoil of the era, he wound up in France, where he attracted students from all over Europe and North America to his complex but brilliant system of transformation, familiarly known as the Work.[20]

The Law of Three, the centerpiece of that system, stipulates that every phenomenon, on every scale (from subatomic to cosmic) and in every domain (physical, sociological, psychospiritual) is the result of the interweaving of three independent forces: the first active (or "affirming," as it's known in the Work), the second passive (or "denying"), and the third neutralizing (or "reconciling"). This is not simply a Hegelian thesis/antithesis/synthesis; the third force is an *independent* line of action, co-equal with the other two, and not simply a *product* of the other two. Just as it takes three strands of hair to make a braid, it takes three individual lines of action to make a new arising. Until this third term enters, the two forces remain at impasse. Once it enters, the situation is catapulted into a whole new ballpark.

Consider a few simple examples. A seed, as Jesus said, "unless it falls into the ground and dies, remains a single seed." If this seed does fall into the ground, it enters a sacred transformative process. *Seed,* the first or affirming force, meets *ground,* the second or denying force (and at that, it has to be *moist* ground, water being its most critical first component). But even in this encounter nothing will happen until *sunlight,* the third, or reconciling force, enters the equation. Among the three they generate a *sprout,*

---

[20] Gurdjieff is most widely known in contemporary spiritual circles as the one who originally introduced the Enneagram to the West, though his understanding of this teaching differs considerably from the prevailing model in the current Enneagram of Personality schools. The Enneagram portrays the interweaving of the Law of Three with the Law of Seven (also known as the Law of World Maintenance) to offer those who can read it a powerful esoteric tool for working with change and process.

which is the actualization of the possibility latent in the seed—and a whole new "field" of possibility.

Or take the analogy of sailing. A sailboat is driven through the water by the interplay of the wind on its sails (first force) and the resistance of the sea against its keel (second force). The result is that the boat is "shot" forward through the water. But as any sailor knows, this schoolbook explanation is not complete. A sailboat, left to its own devices, will not shoot forward through the water; it will round up into the wind and come to a stop. For forward movement to occur, a third force must enter the equation, the heading, or destination, by which the helmsperson determines the proper set of the sail and positioning of the keel. Only if these three are engaged can the desired result emerge, which is the course made good, the actual distance traveled.

In Gurdjieff's Work this law (also known as the Law of World Creation) has been seriously studied for more than eight decades across a wide variety of professional disciplines represented by students of the Work: politicians, scientists, social scientists, philosophers, artists. There is a considerable body of data attesting to the accuracy of this law and its practical effectiveness as a problem solver and impasse breaker. And it continues to be stumbled on by highly credentialed individuals outside of the Work who of course have no idea at what they are staring.[21]

---

[21] A good case in point is the so-called Constructal Law, set forth by Duke University engineering professor Adrian Bejan as a universal cosmic law on the order of the First and Second Laws of Thermodynamics. The Constructal Law is an elegant specific case of the Law of Three. It states: "For a finite-size flow system to persist in time (to live), its configuration must evolve in such a way that provides easier access to the currents that flow through it." In this case the current is affirming force, the structure through which it flows is denying, and the protocol of maximum efficiency is the reconciling force that allows them to meet. The new arising is the design itself, which Bejan has been able to demonstrate always develops a similar and mathematically predictable structure, whether it is the root system of a tree, the capillaries in the lungs, or the architectural engineering of Atlanta's Hartsfield-Jackson International Airport. See Adrian Bejan, *Design in Nature* (New York: Random House, 2012), 3.

But it has never been systematically applied to the Christian doctrine of the Trinity. This is what I set out to do in my 2013 book *The Holy Trinity and the Law of Three*. Taking my cue from Gurdjieff himself, who allusively suggested that "the idea of a third force is found in religion in the concept of the Trinity,"[22] I attempted to apply the basic operating dynamism of the Law of Three—"The interweaving of three forces produces a fourth (the new arising) in a new dimension"—to see how the Trinity might actually carry out its evolutionary work.

The results of my exploration are too complex to summarize here, but essentially I was able to confirm Catherine LaCugna's intuition of a great parabolic curve sweeping from Alpha to Omega along a broadly calculable line of direction. Applying the trinitarian "math" yielded up a cosmic map in seven stages of vastly unequal duration, narrowing to an eye of the needle at the human life of Jesus and then widening back out in two successive aeons marked by increasing spiritual incandescence as they bear down on that point of final implosion already predicted in the calculations. By a very different route I wound up in the same place as Teilhard, in the process creating an unintentional second line of bearing on his crucial mystical insight.

I say "unintentional" because I wrote my book, I confess, before Teilhard was even fully on my radar screen. I did not set out with the goal of confirming his intuitions. But having arrived by my own route, I would say that the only real difference between our paradigms is that what he calls *christogenesis* I would expand to read as "*christogenesis* as the lawful and inevitable progression of the trinitarian evolutionary dynamism."

Ternary Metaphysics

The common denominator in all these distinctly different yet overlapping revisionings is that the Trinity emerges as a metaphysical principle, not merely a theological one. Its major function is

---

[22] Cynthia Bourgeault, *The Holy Trinity and the Law of Three* (Boston: Shambhala Publications, 2013), 36.

to bear witness to "the ultimate triadic structure of reality" and to offer access to this reality both as personal entry point into the mystical body of Christ and as an evolutionary template.

In chapter 5 of *The Holy Trinity and the Law of Three* I offer a new term for the metaphysical roadmap implicit in this emerging understanding of the Trinity: *ternary metaphysics*. Simply put, it is a metaphysical system based on threeness rather than twoness. In place of the static, binary opposites of traditional metaphysics,[23] it offers the inevitable characteristics of threeness: asymmetry, dynamism, an inherent predisposition to innovation, an inherent purposiveness or trajectory, and an *advaita*, or oneness, achieved not through stasis but through dynamic equilibrium.

What happens when we approach Teilhard from this new ternary perspective? For me, the picture looks like tumbler locks falling into place. Many of those critical Teilhardian ideas that remain obscure or even unfathomable in traditional metaphysical categories suddenly become immediately contextualized, and the values Teilhard so passionately championed are essentially identical with those resonating so powerfully here. We might take note particularly of the following points of convergence:

- *Dynamism.* Both Teilhard and the emerging trinitarian metaphysics place primary emphasis on motion, change, and God-as-becoming. The Divine is no longer associated with the timeless and changeless, but with movement, creativity, and self-communication.
- *Evolution.* The trinitarian models here considered confirm that foundational Teilhardian insight of an evolutionary principal woven into the very "stuff of the universe" that ultimately prevails over the force of entropy and leads to progressively more sophisticated differentiation and greater consciousness.

---

[23] By "traditional metaphysics" I am designating not only Scholasticism and Neo-Scholasticism, but also Neoplatonism and that great universal system commonly represented as the Perennial Philosophy.

- *Consistence.* At the heart of Teilhard's lifelong spiritual quest was the search for that ultimate coherence in *quo omnia constant* (in which all things hold together). The portrait emerging from the new trinitarian metaphysics confirms his conviction that the universe is neither random nor insignificant, and that evolution itself, while "groping" its way through chance and recombination, ultimately operates under the sway of a greater unifying principle, which, like a bicycle, remains stable by maintaining forward motion. "Nothing holds together absolutely except through the Whole; and the Whole itself holds together only through its future fulfillment."[24]

- *The heart of matter.* In Teilhard's revolutionary metaphysical vision the evolutionary ascent to the divine fullness—pleromization, in his language—does not lead away from matter, but *through* it. Spirit is no longer a substance but progressively attained as matter is left behind by the organizing principle operative within matter itself, drawing it on to become more and more fully realized, more and more fully itself. The new trinitarian model concurs completely, restoring the *Oikonomia* to center stage as the locus of divine self-communication and matter as a crucial ingredient in these transforming fires.

- *Holographic reciprocity.* What Teilhard means by "pantheism" is paralleled and expanded by Panikkar's "cosmotheandric" and Bruteau's "symbiotic unity." The fundamental idea is that the whole and the part exist in an interabiding unity that together comprise "the dynamism of the real." The whole is not a substance, but a *field of action* generated by this ongoing exchange—"pure relationality," as Panikkar has it.[25]

- *Hyper-personalization.* Through this same relational dynamism, both unity and differentiation are preserved. Advaita, or oneness, is attained not through the reabsorption of

---

[24] Teilhard de Chardin, *Christianity and Evolution*, 71.
[25] Panikkar, *Christophany*, 173.

the part back into the whole (as in classic monism), but rather through an intensifying differentiation that increases capaciousness and hence the profundity of union. Oneness occurs not at the point of utmost simplicity but at the point of utmost complexification. With Bruteau's nuancing factored in, the Trinity emerges as the prototype of this hyper-personalized union, in which identity is preserved (*"inconfuse, immutabilite, indivise, inseparabiliter,"* in the words of Chalcedon) through the continuous intercirculation of kenotic love.

- *Amorization.* In Teilhard's most celebrated quotation he speaks of "harnessing the energy of love." In the new mode of trinitarian reflection, the Trinity becomes the mechanism par excellence for this harnessing of love. Bruteau's brilliant description of why agape love demands three terms and my own work with the Law of Three suggest that threeness is indeed the pathway along which this love must necessarily flow.

- *Convergence.* Of all the great mystical intuitions of Teilhard, this is perhaps the most difficult to verify, even on the new trinitarian map. While a significant number of scientists would now agree that there does indeed seem to be a counter-entropic principle at work in the cosmos, Teilhard's inference that all lines must thereby radiate out from it and converge toward it is by no means established or even demonstrable within the givens of empirical science. And even the ternary systems examined here tend more toward an open-ended evolutionary trajectory (Bruteau) or a dynamic equilibrium (Panikkar). By calling on the predicative capacities of the Law of Three, I am able to confirm Teilhard's intuition of a final convergence.

Teilhard never heard the term *ternary metaphysics,* of course, but it seems that beneath the presenting surface of evolution, what he was actually groping for was something very like this missing threeness. We see a strong foreshadowing of this direction in his intuition of a "third nature" of Christ—"Christ the

Evolver" —through which the risen Christ continues to exercise his cosmogonic agency.[26] From the perspective of the Law of Three, what he seems to be intuitively grappling for is the missing "third force," that missing third term that breaks the stasis and restores forward motion. As scholar James Lyons perceptively notes: "Whereas the Alexandrian Logos was the organizing principle of the stable [that is, binary] Greek cosmos, today we must identify Christ with 'a new Logos': the evolutive principle of a universe in movement."[27] It is this universe in motion that galvanized Teilhard's imagination and inflamed his heart. And it is that universe in motion that ternary metaphysics both invites and impels.

The Ternary Swan

Sixty years after his death Teilhard remains a towering singularity in the world of intellectual thought. People didn't know how to categorize him—and still don't. While he positioned himself primarily as a scientist—and, of course, that was technically correct, since all other professional access points were denied to him by his religious superiors—it has been hard for scientists to claim him as their own, for beyond his immediate domain of paleontology, it is clear that science functions for him primarily as the handmaiden to what can essentially be described as a continuous visionary recital. His leaps are too grand, his navigation beyond the strict boundaries of interdisciplinary rigor too risky, his intuition of a final mystical convergence so adamant that it leaves even his most charitable colleagues in the dust. "Many scientists, as I do, may find it impossible to follow him all the way," admits Julian Huxley in his introduction to *The Phenomenon of Man*.

If he left his fellow scientists scratching their heads, his movements were even more inscrutable to his fellow theologians. His Jesuit confreres silenced and exiled him and have yet to welcome him back fully as one of their most brilliant sons. But

---

[26] For a thoughtful discussion of this "third nature of Christ," see Ilia Delio, *Christ in Evolution* (Maryknoll, NY: Orbis Books, 2008), 76.

[27] James A Lyons, *Cosmic Christ in Origen and Teilhard de Chardin* (London: Oxford University Press, 1982), 185–86.

his rejection is even more sweeping and virulent among contemporary adherents of traditionalist metaphysics, who continue to lambaste him for what are perceived as unpardonable offenses against the classic Neoplatonic roadmap. All those things he was so enamored of—dynamism, uncertainty, complexification, materiality—are inevitably associated with the corrupt and fallen, and wisdom is always and only above (or perhaps *behind*), never in the messy ahead. His open-armed embrace of modernity would seem to be going in exactly the wrong direction, and on that basis he is routinely castigated.

The problem dissolves, I think, when we name Teilhard for what he was and is: a ternary swan in a binary metaphysical duck pond. His lifelong groping along the pathway of evolution was at heart a bold and visionary drive to articulate the inescapable ternary basis of Christian metaphysics and to heal the artificial schism between theology and science, which had only opened up in the first place because the binary roadmap (whether Scholastic or traditionalist), always was, and always will be, too small to accommodate Christianity's intrinsic ternary ground, our most profound treasure from the mind of Christ.

5

The Ecstasy of *Agape*

KERRIE HIDE

God's ecstasy creates the world,
and the world's ecstasy realizes God.
And you are right in the midst of it.
—BEATRICE BRUTEAU, *God's Ecstasy*

I invite you into the pathos of Holy Thursday. Imagine the
Cenacle, a liminal space, a holy of holies where the intimate sharing of love pouring out takes place. It is the evening of the Last
Supper with Jesus. There is a sense of presence and impending
absence, a consciousness of participating in a transfiguring moment in time. Yearning for intimacy, the beloved disciple turns his
back toward Jesus's breast and leans into the heart of Jesus (John
13:23).[1] He returns to the center. Infused in total self-giving, in I-I

---

[1] This is a contemplation that Beatrice encourages. I draw on the
language of "heart" to describe the center of our being, where our identity infuses into Jesus, which is consistent with Beatrice's understanding
of heart. See Beatrice Bruteau, "In the Cave of the Heart: Silence and
Realization," *New Blackfriars* 65 (July/August 1984): 301–19. Jesus
then becomes the "Way" (*hodos)* into Christ, into the Trinity. See Beatrice Bruteau, *Radical Optimism: Rooting Ourselves in Reality* (New
York: Crossroad, 1993), 94.

loving, there is only one love. The beloved disciple becomes one with the subjectivity of Jesus, until there is one heart, one love.

Beatrice explains how this return to the center is as though we begin from the surface of a sphere and retract along a radius toward the point where all the radii meet. As we move beyond our bounded self, back and down and in toward the center, we encounter the heart of Jesus. The consciousness of Jesus becomes available to us. In the words of Beatrice: "We are coming to know the Sacred Heart from the inside, inside his consciousness, and inside our consciousness. And our 'inside' comes to be more and more coincident with his 'inside'. His Heart is becoming the heart of our heart."[2] Through recollecting and centering in our heart in boundless loving, where our heart and the heart of Jesus coincide, we encounter his subjective consciousness of being one in "all in all" (1 Cor 15:28). In love's mutual indwelling we commune in who Jesus is and recognize ourselves in the Ground of all Being, participating in the *enstatic*-ecstatic Trinity.

The intimacy of the infusing of two beloveds has a powerfully attractive energy.[3] In my own journey, as I have entered this timeless contemplation as the beloved over many years, I recognize a movement from desire for oneness to leaning comfortably into Jesus, feeling held, caressed, and embraced, to boundaries merging, as Christ emerges and draws me into the love of the trinitarian inflowing. The flow includes dissolving into darkness, encountering a fear of groundlessness, waiting in unknowing, expanding in boundlessness and trusting the arising of luminous oneness from the groundless ground that constantly reveals a deeper "one-ing". When Teilhard de Chardin plunged

---

[2] Bruteau, *Radical Optimism*, 98.

[3] Teilhard identified two types of energy: tangential, where elements with the same degree of complexity relate; and radial, where elements unite from the center and are drawn forward to higher levels of unification, complexity, consciousness. The energy of *Agape* that Beatrice describes is "radial." It draws from the inside out and creates more complex levels of union. See Beatrice Bruteau, *The Grand Option: Personal Transformation and the New Creation* (Notre Dame, IN: University of Notre Dame Press, 2007), 5.

into the unfathomable abyss of love of the heart of Christ, he saw, in the depthless pools of the eyes of crucified love, an ecstasy of "indescribable agony" and "superabundance of joy" that he once glimpsed in the eyes of a dying soldier.[4] From the luminous vibration of the heart of Jesus, Teilhard recognized the presence of Christ-Omega alluring, personalizing, and unifying the cosmic milieu into greater convergence. Teilhard prophesied: "The light will emerge only when we go deeper. We shall see its radiance only when we leave behind the outer husk of beings and succeed in discovering what is hidden deep within them."[5]

Beatrice takes us beyond the outer husk into the depths of the Heart. She opens a pathway through the confines of our egoic mind into the non-dual consciousness of our Essential Self,[6] to evolve in consciousness and awaken "communion" consciousness. She invites us into the involution that empowers evolution, so we may live in the ground of the ecstasy of *Agape*, of God creating the world and the world realizing God: Live from the ground of the ecstasy of *Agape*. Live in the middle, the center, the core, the hub of our divine life. This is the invitation Beatrice Bruteau offers the world through her life, her writings, and the mystical spirit she now empowers in the noosphere, the realm of mind or consciousness. Influenced by the timeless wisdom of Vedanta, by her study of mathematics and philosophy, by Jewish mysticism, and by being immersed in the wisdom of Sri Aurobindo and Teilhard de Chardin, Beatrice claimed her identity as a mystic. She pondered deeply the mystery of our place

---

[4] Pierre Teilhard de Chardin, "Christ in the World of Matter," *Hymn of the Universe,* trans. Simon Bartholomew (London: Collins, 1965), 45–46. Christ-Omega is the one heart, the fully integrated "person" at the center of all.

[5] Pierre Teilhard de Chardin, *Science and Christ,* trans. René Hague (New York: Harper and Row, 1968), 23.

[6] This center of pure oneness is beyond all names. In Hindu it is our "Absolute Self," in Zen Buddhism it is our "Original Face," for the Taoists our "Original Nature." Beatrice Bruteau, "Prayer and Identity," in Thomas Keating et al., *Spirituality, Contemplation, and Transformation: Writings on Centering Prayer* (New York: Lantern Books, 2008), 85–86.

in the origins of the cosmos. Her writings create a spaciousness for us now, at this time of evolution in this second axial period, to see how, as Ilia Delio suggests, theology is born from mystical insight.[7] Beatrice awakens the original vision of our being in God so that we may discover ourselves as one in this great, evolving, birthing of God as cosmos.

In this chapter, after seeing how Beatrice envisages *Agape* as divine ecstasy, we explore how God creates the world in the ecstasy of *Agape* and the world's ecstasy realizes God. We focus on the three essential icons that Beatrice develops: Trinity, Incarnation, and the universe as Theotokos or God-bearer.[8] In response, we consider the awakening of consciousness that is necessary for us to live in the midst of the *enstatic*-ecstatic flow of love and evolve in harmony with divine becoming.

God's Ecstasy

God Is Agape

Deep in our heart we are filled with ecstatic longing for oneness with the Absolute. We yearn to know the Ground of Being, to experience meaningful wholeness, and to encounter love in our life. Beatrice responds to these stirrings by immersing us in the fecundity of divine Love. In *Easter Mysteries* she asks "What is love?" and explores *ho theos agape estin* (God is love) (1 John 4:8; 4:16). In response, conscious of keeping language soft, pliable, and suggestive,[9] Beatrice chooses to remain with the Greek *agape* so she may distinguish the personal nature of the absolute

---

[7] Ilia Delio, *Christ in Evolution* (Maryknoll, NY: Orbis Books, 2008), 102.

[8] Theotokos is the title given to Mary at the Counsel of Ephesus (431 CE). It celebrates Mary's giving birth to God.

[9] Beatrice Bruteau, *God's Ecstasy: The Creation of a Self-Creating World* (New York: Crossroad, 1997), 35.

fullness of the sharing of divine Love.[10] She highlights that *agape* is not a response. Nor is it a divine attribute. God *is Agape*. God cannot be God without being *Agape*.[11] God-*Agape* is personal, intimate, self-disclosing and self-giving. God-*Agape* is the bountiful Love-energy that is existence. Endless, without origin, without source, *Agape* arises from emptiness, from nothing.[12] It is prevenient, unconditional, loving because Love loves. *Agape* is intimate creative union that "ones" as it seeks the fullness of love. It is the fire of Love-energy that is at the core of evolution that Teilhard urges us to harness. *Agape* is who we are.

Enstatic-Ecstatic

Arising from the depths of *Agape's* passion for uniting, ecstasy is the release of Love-energy. In mystical theology *ekstasis* is associated with Paul's experience: "I live, yet not I, but Christ lives in me" (Gal 2:20).[13] *Ecstasy* denotes passion, intoxication, extreme joy, sexual pleasure. It encapsulates the enflaming experience of mystical union, of being drawn beyond oneself, floating in endless expanse in the mystery of Love's boundlessness. The fluidity of the term enables it to hold the experience of transcendence in union with God. Whether we dissolve in darkness, or are filled with light, ecstasy describes expanding beyond the

---

[10] Beatrice makes a distinction between *Agape* and Eros, suggesting that Eros seeks pleasure for the one giving. I suggest envisaging Eros as desire with the potential to harness sexual energy in perichoresis. See, for example, Douglas Christi, *The Blue Sapphire of the Mind* (New York: Oxford, 2013), 225–68.

[11] Beatrice Bruteau, *The Easter Mysteries* (New York: Crossroad, 1995), 59.

[12] *Nothing* means "no quality, attribute, direction, or preference." It signifies that there is no concept or word for the original or underlying. See Bruteau, *God's Ecstasy*, 84.

[13] See *The New Dictionary of Catholic Spirituality,* ed. Michael Downey (Collegeville, MN: Liturgical Press, 1993), 333–34. For a history of ecstasy in philosophy see Dorothee Soelle, *The Silent Cry: Mysticism and Resistance* (New York: Fortress Press, 2001), 27–44.

mind, releasing all boundaries, feeling lost in another, becoming no-thing. Paradoxically, as Dorothee Soelle observes, "it is precisely in stepping out that ecstasy is the most inward of all."[14] Beatrice identifies this profound inwardness as *enstasy*.

Enstasy denotes pure transcendence, the exquisite inner tranquillity of being grounded and remaining within one-self.[15] It is primordial oneness, the energy-less energy of the shimmering stillness of pure silence. It is *nada*, nothing, the absolute. *Enstasy* marks the singularity, the point in mathematics where all representation breaks down into infinity. It evokes the most inner pointless point.[16] And like ecstasy that is most inward when it burgeons out, *enstasy* marks the pressure point that inflates and pours forth as radiant ecstasy. *Enstasy*-ecstasy flows as one reality. Beatrice likens this flow to quantum fluctuations oscillating between physical nothingness and something-ness, appearance and annihilation.[17] Beyond any physical or metaphysical cause, beyond motive, God is *enstatic* and ecstatic. The *kenosis* of the Philippian hymn (Phil 2:6) expresses the lovely interplay of *enstasy*-ecstasy. Though God is *enstatic* as formless *Agape*, God does not remain in *enstatis*, transcendently within God's self; God empties out, manifests, taking the form of a servant (the cosmos), pouring forth love, enabling the formless to take form in the finite.[18] Beatrice further likens the dynamism of *enstasy*-ecstasy to dancing, because "the dance is precisely the dance in the act of dancing."[19] Like Shiva Nataraja's cosmic encircling

---

[14] Soelle, *Silent Cry*, 3.

[15] Bruteau, *God's Ecstasy*, 27.

[16] Ibid., 84. *Enstatis* is used to describe Samadhi or the attainment of pure awareness in Hinduism. See Abishiktananda, *Prayer* (Noida: ISPC, 2001).

[17] Bruteau, *God's Ecstasy*, 84.

[18] Ibid., 9–10.

[19] Ibid., 39; see also Bruteau, *Radical Optimism*, 137n.1 where she likens this to Aslan, the lion who sings the world into existence in C. S. Lewis's *Chronicles of Narnia* (London: HarperCollins, 1950–56), and to the dance of tribal Africans described in Lyall Watson's *Lightening Bird* (London: Coronet, 1983), where the dancers become the animal they are dancing.

dance, the infinite dance of *enstatic*-ecstatic energy joyfully expands outward, as the inside dancers turn into the outside-ness of the dance. The dance is *enstatic*-ecstatic *Agape*.

Icon of the Trinity

In this dance of *Agape,* Trinity becomes an icon of the dynamism of the gracious exchange of love-energy. In contrast to classical metaphysics, which distinguishes between the divine substance and divine relating, Beatrice develops a philosophy of *Being*, resonant with Orthodox theology and the evolutionary view of Teilhard, that: "what comes first in the world for our thought is not 'being' but 'the union which produces this being.'"[20] It is not substance but the interrelationship of communion among persons that is at the heart of reality. Though the language of *person* can confuse, for Beatrice, to be a person is to be "an act of loving," a process, a flow of *Agape*.[21] Beatrice affirms: "If God is love, then God must be a 'quest for union,' for oneness. The love-relations must be intrinsic to the oneness, must be total self-givings that are mutual indwellings, drawing all into a vital, a living oneness."[22] In order for love to flow there must be a minimum of three persons, so that the Self-giving is total, mutual indwelling as one and many.[23] The

---

[20] Pierre Teilhard de Chardin, *Christianity and Evolution*, trans. René Hague (New York: Harcourt, 1971), 227. Cf. Ilia Delio, *The Unbearable Wholeness of Being* (Maryknoll, NY: Orbis Books, 2013), 44–45.

[21] This phrase is from Daniel Walsh. In keeping with Walsh, Beatrice defines *person* as formless, unborn, immortal, transcendental and co-extensive with being. It is in nature and personality that personal characteristics are formed. See Beatrice Bruteau, "The One and the Many: Communitarian Nondualism," in *The Other Half of My Soul: Bede Griffiths and the Hindu-Christian Dialogue,* comp. Beatrice Bruteau (Wheaton: Quest Books, 1996), 268–75.

[22] Bruteau, *God's Ecstasy*, 36.

[23] Beatrice stresses that to be one the Trinity must be at least three persons in order to exchange love energy. Three represents many. See Bruteau, *God's Ecstasy*, 34. Cynthia Bourgeault points to the importance of this dynamic expressed in the rule of three (*The Holy Trinity and the Law of Three: Discovering the Radical Truth at the Heart of Christianity* [Boston: Shambhala, 2013], 87).

persons remain within themselves in *enstasy*, yet simultaneously express their differentiated identity giving themselves ecstatically, creating perichoresis, an encircling dance of one in another.[24] Encircling and interpenetrating creates endless "one-ing," infinite Presence in Presence, exquisite *circumincession*.[25] The Trinity-Lovers pour out their hearts into one another as one and many, forming a communion of Wholeness-Oneness.

What is crucial in this encircling *Agape* is the intimate, personal nature of *Being*. Drawing on the foundational work of Martin Buber,[26] who made a distinction between an "I-It" subject-object relationship that sees the other as separate, and an "I-Thou," face-to-face relationship, where love is encountered and received from the other, Beatrice explores how the interrelating of trinitarian *Agape* is "I-I," subject to subject.[27] In the encircling perichoresis, each Lover gives Self to the other person in ecstasy, unites in the Loved One's *enstasy*, and together as one, they love the third Beloved. The three persons become one "I." This "I" is the luminous light revealed on Mt. Sinai, the fire of the "I am" that enflames the burning bush (Exod 3:2), Pure Presence, Absolute Being. The encircling *enstatic*-ecstatic burgeoning of one in another continues. Each Lover loves totally. Each is both Lover and Beloved. Each is both one and many. The whole Trinity is an exchange of creative union, one in another in communion.

---

[24] *Perichoresis* is the Greek term introduced by John Damascene to highlight the dynamic and vital character of each divine person as well as the coherence and immanence of each person in the other two. See Catherine Mowry LaCugna, *God for Us: The Trinity and Christian Life* (San Francisco: HarperSanFrancisco, 1991), 270.

[25] *Circumincession* is the Latin term meaning "circling." See Bruteau, *The Grand Option*, 56.

[26] Martin Buber, *I and Thou* (New York: Scribner, 1957). See also Bruteau, *God's Ecstasy*, 30. It is noteworthy that Buber speaks of ecstasy as coming from bursting through the commotion of the world to find the oneness within, which in turn draws us without (*Ecstatic Confessions*, ed. Paul Mendes Flohr, trans. Esther Cameron [San Francisco: Harper and Row, 1985], 1). See also Soelle, *Silent Cry*, 30–31.

[27] Bruteau, *God's Ecstasy*, 31.

Each says to the other: "May you be."[28] Each imparts pure, conscious, creative, dynamic *Agape*. This same encircling dance of Love, Beloved, Lover exchanging *Agape* naturally overflows into creation. *Agape* incarnates, becomes flesh through speaking the Word into creation, and God's ecstasy creates the world.

God's Ecstasy Creates the World

Icon of Incarnation

From within this dynamic of ecstatic *Agape*, the second icon of incarnation reveals the Christic nature of ecstasy. Crucially for Beatrice, in keeping with Franciscan soteriology,[29] incarnation does not occur because creation went astray. Rather, incarnation is an organic expression of the Trinity's endless self-sharing. Beatrice explores this incarnational dynamic through exegeting John 1:18: "No one has ever seen God; the only begotten God who is in the *(kolpon—hollow)* of the Father, that one *(exehesato—exegetes)*."[30] In other words, from the "unseen" *kolpon* (hollow, womb, heart, emptiness, no-thing), flows the only begotten One, the Word. Always grounded in the Heart-*kolpon*, the enfleshed Word exegetes, breathes, speaks, devises ways to express eternal Love in space-time. The transcendent becomes visible as "real" Presence, as cosmos. And, just as the Trinity expresses love, one to the other, the Word says in creation: "May you be."[31] What is

---

[28] Ibid., 29.

[29] See Delio, *Christ in Evolution*, 53–65.

[30] Bruteau, *God's Ecstasy*, 38. In *The Grand Option*, 124, Beatrice draws on language resonate with an interfaith context. The root of reality, source or parent of all, conceives and expresses itself breathing forth a meaning, a Word. The Word is the form that the Holy Breath takes as it issues from the source. The Word also takes on flesh in the world so that the self-expression of the infinite takes on finite form. The full reality of incarnate deity is both infinite and finite, formless and possessing form.

[31] Bruteau, *God's Ecstasy*, 38.

spoken, Beatrice affirms is "truly, wholly and thoroughly 'God' and truly wholly and thoroughly 'cosmos.'"[32] In the tradition of Teilhard, the Word holds the ecstasy of the divine, human, and cosmic, creating an evolutionary dance of *Agape*.[33]

Life Evolving

Subsequently, Beatrice explores how the ecstasy of the Word into creation is not a first cause in the sense of initiating a process separate from divine life. The ecstasy in which creation evolves is divine life loving. The dynamic is intrinsically *enstatic*-ecstatic, with self-creating held within natural laws, because divine creativity is the prototype for uniting and diversifying. Imbedded in perichoresis, creation holds an innate desire to unite and form new levels of "creative union."[34] Drawing on her extensive scientific background, Beatrice demonstrates how creation continues to be incarnational in self-creating as the embryonic energy of space-time evolves. She enhances a sense of wonder at the original creative unifying moment when chaos, space, and light inflate and produce the energy that contains the foundations of matter. Fundamental principles of the universe emerge with the inherent capacity to fertilize and create more fecundity. Stars, planets, and expanding galaxies form as randomness reconfigures into intricate patterns that enhance the potential of life.[35] In enstatic "inflation," atoms unite and form molecules. Molecules unite and form cells.[36] The union of cells creates organisms, with the same

---

[32] Ibid., 139.

[33] See Teilhard, *Christianity and Evolution*, 179. Aurobindo speaks of three "poises" of the Absolute: transcendent, cosmic, and individual (see Bruteau, *Radical Optimism*, 138n.1).

[34] Creative union occurs when elements unite with equal value and dignity and form another level of complexity bringing into being something that never existed before. See Bruteau, *The Grand Option*, 3–4.

[35] See Bruteau, *God's Ecstasy*, 58–81. This is not pantheism, which limits God to the universe, but rather more panentheism, which sees everything within the being of God who is transcendently Absolute.

[36] For details of the symbiotic chemistry that evolves, see ibid., 87–109.

pattern of creative union occurring at each level of organization. Risk and "unknowability" are intrinsic because they radiate from self-abandoning love. Instability, randomness, and chaos create the potential for the expansion of being. Through variation and natural selection, sameness and difference continually expand in *Agape's* ecstasy. *Agape* unfurls as evolution.

As the universe story unfolds in the perichoresis of *Agape*, more conscious beings form from the creative union of less complex and less conscious elements. Plant and animal species evolve, with each new species preparing the foundations for self-reflective consciousness to develop in human beings. In the evolution of consciousness we are on the threshold of having a renewed sense of the incarnational nature of the cosmos in realizing God. With the creative freedom of Spirit that flows in human beings through oneness in the Word, humankind has a crucial evolutionary role in enabling the world's ecstasy to realize God.

The World's Ecstasy Realizes God

Icon of Theotokos

The lavish potential of *Agape's* incarnating presence within the world illuminates the third icon that Beatrice develops: the universe as Theotokos, or God-bearer.[37] Paul's seminal metaphor of birthing holds the dynamic. "The whole of creation has been groaning in labour pains . . . until now . . . with eager longing for the emergence of the children of God" (Rom 8:22, 19).[38] In creation we see the fullness of trinitarian love incarnating and birthing divine offspring through creation creating. Beatrice quotes the Talmud: "Who has Wisdom?" She responds: "The one who sees the unborn."[39] We are called to see the unborn,

---

[37] Beatrice adopts the title Theotokos or God-bearer, suggesting its virtues lie in its ability to carry paradox, reversal and closure. The Theotokos is a creature born of God who then becomes the mother of God (ibid., 21).

[38] Ibid., 174. This is Beatrice's translation.

[39] Ibid., 176.

to cherish and foster what is deeply within the *enstasy* of the universe and midwife future abundance. As the *enstatic* within creation releases ecstatically, the cycle of encircling perichoresis manifests. We bear God. This, Beatrice identifies as the trinitarian lifecycle that flows from Transcendent to Incarnate to Realized.[40] Realizing this incarnating creativity is crucial for our future.

Agape Suffering

The existential question of the intensity of the agony of the pain of labor that naturally occurs or even seems opposed to creation's birthing of divine life confronts us. In a world so torn with violence and division this vision of oneness in divine life can even seem naive.[41] Yet, it is from deep within existential despair and meaninglessness, when life throws us into chaos, that the Word stirs in the ground of our heart and arises in love. When the mystery of the Word speaking love in the midst of suffering touches our hearts in the darkness, heart consciousness awakens. Absence illumines a fuller sense of presence. In the words of Teilhard we realize that "we are evolution."[42] We can take the "grand option," creatively choosing to become conscious of who we truly are as divine creative love incarnate and evolve. We can nurture our Christic nature and become the Word spoken from the inner life of trinitarian loving and give birth to divinity. It is crucial, Beatrice prophesies, for us to be conscious enough to realize that this awakening is the Theotokos returning to the Ground of all Being in our own experience of being the ground

---

[40] Ibid.

[41] For Beatrice, suffering is pain or injury and the compassionate desire that this should not be. How we choose to live in our own and others' suffering changes the nature of suffering. Evil is caught up in reaction, in the "karma trap." It is not the opposite of Goodness, which originates from pure being. Evil always refers to something and operates as a choice or reaction that alienates. Evil is never an original creative act. See Bruteau, *The Grand Option*, 70–73.

[42] Pierre Teilhard de Chardin, *The Phenomenon of Man*, trans. Bernard Wall (New York: Harper, 1959), 231. See also Bruteau, *The Grand Option*, 83.

incarnated as cosmos.[43] In returning to the ground of our heart we find ourselves, intimately part of incarnation, living in the midst of ecstasy.

In the Midst of Ecstasy

As Amicus-Friend

Again, I invite you to return to the contemplation of Holy Thursday.[44] Notice how in the symbolic self-giving of Jesus, consciousness evolved. In the ritual outpouring of Jesus washing feet and sharing his body and blood, the revelation on Mt. Sinai of Wholeness-Oneness is fulfilled. The entrenched hierarchical paradigm of Lord-servant transforms into *Amicus*-Friend. In order for us to live consciously in the fullness of *Amicus*-Friend, Beatrice envisages that the next moment in our evolution is to sink into the depths of our own consciousness, into the heart of the risen Christ, into the *enstasis* of "I." As we coincide in the center of Jesus and recognize our origins in the infusing exchange of the *enstasy*-ecstasy of divine community of *Agape*, our risen Christic identity arises. Through entwining and "one-ing" our will with the divine will,[45] and seeing through the one "eye" that we, all together, are the one "I," we infuse all other heart centers. Realization and responsiveness to this interchange of heart energy is crucial for our future evolving.

Into the Center

This journey into this non-dualistic way of seeing takes us to our limits and beyond. It is in the vulnerability of many heartbreaks and dyings that emptiness, absence, and nothingness reveal their

---

[43] Bruteau, *God's Ecstasy,* 177.

[44] Beatrice Bruteau, *Holy Thursday Revolution* (Maryknoll, NY: Orbis Books, 2005), 53.

[45] *Will* is the term Beatrice adopts, which I prefer to translate as our "active loving" or "desire." Here we see how Beatrice integrates the Eastern stress on consciousness and the Western stress on will, again taking us beyond dualism.

enstatic fertility. Through living the paschal mystery of dying and rising in Christ, surrendering our self-descriptions and attachments into the poverty of naked simplicity, passing from depth to depth in the abyss of our heart, we discover *enstasy*, our original Heart-Self one in luminous Christ-*Omega*. We awaken in our "resurrection body."[46] Beyond words, images and feelings, in the obscurity of unknowing,[47] we see, through resurrection eyes, that we participate in *Agape's* ecstasy.[48] Christ-consciousness awakens. In participatory loving knowledge,[49] intuited from the luminous dark ground of the source of consciousness itself,[50] the "eye" of our heart sees from oneness, from perichoresis, from the intimacy of encircling, indwelling love-energy.

Beatrice celebrates this naked reality that contemplation exposes when she describes contemplation as "a movement of consciousness from God, with God in God *as* God out into the world, a movement in which the divine consciousness and

---

[46] Beatrice Bruteau,"Eucharistic Ecology and Ecological Spirituality," *Crosscurrents* 40/4 (Winter 1990–91), 491. Christ-Omega is *the* Heart of all reality, the fully integrated "person," beyond boundaries of religion.

[47] In Bruteau, *Radical Optimism*, 157. Beatrice highlights the dualism between the two extremes of observing our inner heart: "reflexive" and "negation determination." "Reflexive" consciousness actively observes and distinguishes. "Negation determination" abandons the inner-observer witnessing what we are doing interiorly. She encourages a third integrated way of seeing through embodying the fullness of our being, noetically coinciding with our Self by experiencing our own existence interiorly beyond subject-object. This I am calling "heart consciousness." I adopt the term *heart consciousness* to emphasize how this consciousness flows when we are centered in the "heart" of our being. See Bruteau, "Prayer and Identity," 107. Heart consciousness is not a psychic state, but a metaphysical perception that comes when we shift our identity into our heart.

[48] See Bruteau, "Eucharistic Ecology and Ecological Spirituality," 499–515.

[49] For some significant implications of this form of participatory knowledge, see Constance Fitzgerald, "Transformation in Wisdom," in *Carmel and Contemplation: Transforming Human Consciousness,* ed. Kevin Culligan and Regis Jordan, 341–42 (Washington: ICS, 2000).

[50] Bruteau, "Prayer and Identity," 108.

my consciousness, flowing together, stream out in love and in creative, healing, beautifying energy."[51] In claiming our identity in the Word, nestled in the Heart-*kolpon* of the Absolute and graciously enfleshed in holy sensuality, we trace our reality back to the sharing of love of "I-I" becoming "I am." The "one-ing" is so interpenetrating, we see "from," "with," "in" and *"as"* God.[52] Beatrice identifies the *enstatic* energy that erupts as "spondic." Like the radiance of a "solar eclipse," the energy that emanates is powerfully luminous.[53] In her words, "We no sooner touch the "still point" at the core our being, this immutable at the heart of mutability, than we discover it as an explosion of energy."[54] *Agape* pours out like a "sacred libation."[55] Its power explodes into seeking further union, pouring out compassion, hallowing all it touches, saying "May you be."[56] Beatrice stresses that "spiritual life does not end with . . . union with the Absolute. Rather, it is where it begins."[57] Union with the Absolute is the originating principle, not where we end. Realizing that we are incarnating transcendent energy centers activates communion consciousness.

In Communion Consciousness

Communion consciousness[58] awakens as we enter into the ground of our heart, recover our original memory of being one

---

[51] Bruteau, *Radical Optimism*, 132.

[52] Consciousness is awareness. Wayne Teasdale, a friend of Beatrice's, suggests that all we experience is represented to us through consciousness: "Consciousness is the inside, outside, nearside and far side of reality; it is the height, breadth and transcendent beyond." See Wayne Teasdale, *The Mystic Heart: Discovering Universal Spirituality in the World Religions* (Novato: New World Library, 2001), 65. In Hinduism, Brahman is consciousness. The Trinity is consciousness, fully consciousness of all.

[53] Bruteau, "Prayer and Identity," 108.

[54] Bruteau, *The Grand Option*, 52.

[55] See ibid., 2–57.

[56] Bruteau, "Prayer and Identity," 99.

[57] Bruteau, *The Grand Option*, 124.

[58] It is important to note that "communion" consciousness is formed in the center of the Heart and is more actively seeking union than the "collective" consciousness that we participate in the unconsciousness.

in Christ, and stabilize in the organic identity of our participation in the ecstasy of the Trinity. We realize that we are luminous, spondic centers of consciousness, one with other centers in the one Spirit-filled body of Christ. We can draw on pure Spirit, choose to activate our will, and unite with other spondic centers. As we align our center with the *enstatic* center of others,[59] a new level of bonded heart energy forms in Omega, a communal "mind" of Christ that manifests as *Amicus*-communion. "Communion" consciousness provides a way to move forward in advancing the complexification of religious consciousness, in what Ilia Delio identifies as the task of the second axial period, to form a consciousness of relatedness that is global, transcultural, integral.[60] This will occur, Beatrice suggests, when we unite in heart-centered consciousness. It is only from within the naked "I am" in the depths of the one heart, Omega, that a new level of creative union, of I-I relating can form that is truly inclusive. Humanity becomes a new creation.

Plunging into the depths of evolving consciousness in the wholeness of Christ, activating our human energies and stabilizing our identity in the *enstatic*-ecstatic interpenetration of *Agape,* heightens awareness of the universe as Theotokos. The fertility of communion in "I am" necessarily extends to creation, releasing an "ecological" consciousness,[61] informed by the heartbeat

---

[59] This movement of communion consciousness resonates with Teilhard's "Reflections on Happiness," where he describes the movement from "centering" in ourselves, emerging from ourselves by "decentering" and uniting ourselves with others in such a way as to develop through the union an added measure of consciousness. We then realize the necessity to expand into the "super-centration" of circles of ever increasing radius. We belong to one single great humanity that is animated by one single heart united in loving (Pierre Teilhard de Chardin, *Toward the Future,* trans. René Hague [New York: Harcourt Brace Jovanovich, 1975], 116–20). This sense of evolving human nature is also consistent with Aurobindo's vision that a new humanity will form through the divine consciousness coming to fuller awareness in humanity. See Roy Posner, *An Analysis of Sri Aurobindo's The Divine Life* (2015), electronic book.

[60] Delio, *Christ in Evolution,* 177.

[61] See Bruteau, "Eucharistic Ecology and Ecological Spirituality," 499–515.

of creation. Aware that we are one living being, one "I am" in Christ, *Agape* ecstatically dancing, we can say with creation: "I am the earth. I am the sea. I am the air we breathe." Consciousness becomes what Beatrice identifies as "Wholistic,"[62] a capacity to see from within the wholeness of organic being, to desire the "one thing necessary" (Luke 10:42), the fullness of life for all in all. This conscious evolution celebrates the "one-ing" of all things in God that Julian of Norwich beheld. Teilhard's envisioning of the coming to consciousness of Omega in the noosphere (the communal heart-mind) enhances.[63] David Bohm's sense of holographic presence that we are wholes, within wholes, within wholes, becomes our reality. In the exchange of love in communion consciousness, we further the perichoresis of the Trinity as ecstatic Lovers birthing divine newness.

Living as Ecstatic Lovers

Thich Nhat Hanh says that "the bells of mindfulness are sounding," calling us to be attentive, to wake up and listen.[64] The editor of *Spiritual Ecology*, Llewellyn Vaughan-Lee, urges us to respond as the earth wails in labor pains because we have forgotten and lost the sacred in all things.[65] Yet, as Rumi asks so poignantly in affirming the power of *Agape*, repeating the words of Jesus to Mary Magdalene: "Why do you weep?" (John 21:13).

> *That source is within you*
> *And this whole world is springing up from it.*
> *The source is full,*
> *Its waters are ever flowing:*
> *Do not grieve,*
> *Drink your fill!*

---

[62] Bruteau, *The Grand Option*, 86.

[63] Pierre Teilhard de Chardin, *Human Energy*, trans. J. M. Cohen (New York: Harcourt, Brace, Jovanovich, 1971), 160.

[64] Thich Nhat Hanh, "The Bells of Mindfulness," in *Spiritual Ecology: The Cry of the Earth*, ed. Llewellyn Vaughan-Lee, 25–28 (Point Reyes, CA: The Golden Sufi Centre, 2013), 25.

[65] Vaughan-Lee, *Spiritual Ecology*, v.

> *Don't think it will ever run dry,*
> *This is the endless Ocean.*[66]

Our world is living Being, *enstatic*-ecstatic love energy, an endless Ocean of *Agape* dancing. Yet questions resound and echo. Will *Agape* dance freely in consciousness? Will the ecstasy of God as cosmos be fully recognized? Will the heart of the world be heard? Beatrice suggests that although we cannot lay out a precise structure for the future of our world, we can have hope in the fullness of *Agape* and the innate goodness of human beings. When we return to the ground of our heart, we can predict that the next phase of the world will be a paradigm of perichoresis.[67] The humanity of tomorrow is emerging from the midst of a future in God's ecstasy. With eloquence Beatrice reassures us:

> And so after withdrawing from our sense of limited identity with a restricted self, after realization of our transcendence and freedom and our nature as ecstatic lovers who enter the profound union of non-dual perichoresis, we turn our faces outward again in the creative process of incarnation.[68]

We now participate in a growing body of people evolving with the capacity to return to the ground of the Heart and live in the perichoresis of Love's Trinity. We are recognizing our Christic nature and turning the face of our heart outward to incarnate creatively the fullness of *Agape* dancing. We do know that we are one. We are inter-connected and participate in the consciousness of creation and are sensitizing to the consciousness of earth, of all living things, of galaxies, and of the entire transcendental cosmic awareness. We realize we are integral in the process of

---

[66] Jonathan Star and Shahram Shiva, *A Garden Beyond Paradise: The Mystical Poetry of Rumi* (New York: Bantam Books, 1992), 148–49.

[67] Bruteau, *The Grand Option*, 62.

[68] Ibid., 25.

conscious evolution. Our conscious choices will affect our future irrevocably. Beatrice shows us a path into *Agape*, into the divine awareness where all levels of awareness are held within the exquisite flow of the ecstasy of *Agape*. As we behold the three icons Beatrice illuminates—Trinity, incarnation, and Theotokos—many implications emerge. I highlight three fundamental movements.

First, contemplative prayer is essential to the evolutionary process. As Teilhard foresaw, it is only when we "harness for God the energies of love"[69] that we will discover the fire of love's evolving. This involves a radical *kenosis* of choosing to enter the ground of the heart and risk living in the placeless place of Love's endlessness. It demands the courage to expand into the *enstatic*-ecstatic desire to love others into being. Our role at present is to go within and stabilize in our heart, in the one Heart, and intentionally flow in harmony with *enstatic*-ecstatic *Agape*. This does not mean that those who do not see and respond, or who feel lost, abandoned, or afraid, are left behind—on the contrary. The conscious pouring out of *Agape* of one person strengthens the whole. All are held and affected by the compassionate pouring out of love. In contemplation we meet in our shared poverty and vulnerability in the one Heart of God in center to center oneness. Mindful participation in the evolutionary desire for harmony and wholeness enhances hope in a future where the exquisite dance of love begetting love becomes our full reality.

Second, we are at the threshold of a new participatory love-knowledge, a communal awareness that is arising from returning to the groundless ground of Heart consciousness. We are being summoned to see from oneness, to surrender into deeper ways of perichoresis, of *enstatic*-ecstatic being one-in-another. This means claiming our oneness in the communion of Love's Trinity and seeing together from abundance, rather than seeing from constraint and scarcity. From this fullness of being truly loved, we can then love others in center-to-center oneness. The ability to see from wholeness, to seek what unites, becomes the human norm. Communion consciousness is trustworthy. It is truly discerning in

---

[69] Teilhard, *Toward the Future*, 87.

revealing a way through the impasse of the divisions that non-dual consciousness has thrust upon the world, into the mind of Christ (1 Cor 2:16) where all is one. This awakening of a universal mystical consciousness is not for a select few. It belongs to us all. We all have the potential to see "from," "with," "in," and "*as*" God together and continue incarnating divine life.

Third, the whole universe is God's ecstasy. We are one dynamic extravagant glorious single living Being. The whole universe is imprinted with the same desire to share being, to unite creatively and form new ways of being as Love's Trinity, bringing Love's reality to conscious expression. As we behold the abundance of *Agape's enstasy*-ecstasy still unfurling in creation and enable creation to speak through our consciousness, a new abundance is emerging. Beatrice lived the abundance.

We, lovers formed in the *enstatic*-ecstatic Trinity, can evolve by pouring ourselves into the liquid radiance of love and crying: "This is my body, this is my blood." Through entering the abyss of our heart, releasing and ecstatically flowing beyond all limitations into the vibrancy of *Agape,* we find the Holy Wholeness, the One, the All. In the communion consciousness of Beatrice and Abishiktananda, Beatrice writes, "Nothing remains but being . . . being pure light, undivided infinite light, light itself, the glory of being, the fullness of all joy . . . the Joy of being, God all in all."[70] We are the ecstasy of *Agape.*

---

[70] Bruteau, *Radical Optimism,* 102.

6

Evolution toward Personhood

ILIA DELIO, OSF

The new cosmology has evoked a radically new understanding of the human person, one that significantly differs from the static categories of the past. There is no writer who grasped this more comprehensively than Pierre Teilhard de Chardin. The Jesuit scientist saw a deep compatibility between Christian faith and evolution and described evolution as the grand narrative of cosmic life. Evolution, he claimed, is ultimately a progression toward consciousness. Biological evolution begins on the level of physical convergence and increases in complexity and consciousness. The openness of evolution toward new and complex life undergirds the maxim: life prefers increased life.

For Teilhard, consciousness is not a distinct human phenomenon but active at all levels of reality. The mental enters the material reality in a natural way. He considered matter and consciousness not as two substances or two different modes of existence but as two aspects of the same cosmic stuff. The within is the mental aspect and the without is the physical aspect of the same stuff; physical and psychic are co-related in the evolutionary movement of convergence and complexity.[1] He links evolution of

---

[1] Pierre Teilhard de Chardin, *The Phenomenon of Man*, trans. Bernard Wall (New York: Harper and Row, 1959), 62–64.

the mind with physical and psychic energy. The human person is integrally part of evolution in that we rise from the process, but in reflecting on the process we stand apart from it. He defines reflection as "the power acquired by consciousness to turn in upon itself, to take possession of itself *as an object* . . . no longer merely to know, but to know that one knows."[2] The human person is "the point of emergence in nature at which this deep cosmic evolution culminates and declares itself,"[3] that is, from which self-reflective thought is born.

In 1940 Teilhard completed his most important work, *The Phenomenon of Man*, in which he described the fourfold sequence of the evolution of galaxies, earth, life, and consciousness. The human person is not a ready-made fact but the outflow of billions of years of evolution, beginning with cosmogenesis and the billions of years that led to biogenesis. He saw evolution of the human person as part of the whole natural process of creativity and generativity. Evolution is not a background to the human story; it *is* the human story. The human person is not the great exception to evolution but its recapitulation. Convergent evolution is directed toward a projected point of maximum human organization and consciousness. Through the meandering process of evolution consciousness unfolds through the activities of complexification and convergence. Elements are drawn together and, as they are, new levels of relationships are formed. Consciousness is, in a basic sense, the flow of information across complex levels of relationships; the greater the degrees of relationship, the greater the levels of informational flow. Hence, convergence is the ongoing process of complexification, and the process of convergence and complexity form the necessary conditions for the rise of consciousness in evolution.[4]

---

[2] Ibid., 165.

[3] Pierre Teilhard de Chardin, *Human Energy*, trans. J. M. Cohen (New York: Harcourt, Brace, Jovanovich, 1969), 23.

[4] Pierre Teilhard de Chardin, *Christianity and Evolution*, trans. René Hague (New York: Harcourt, Brace, Jovanovich, 1971), 87.

Teilhard described evolution of the human person as part of the natural process of creativity and generativity. Contrary to the biblical literalists, the human species did not descend from a single couple named Adam and Eve; nor was the human person fully formed by God and placed on earth less than ten thousand years ago. According to a recent Gallup Poll, 42 percent of the US population believes in special creation, while 31 percent maintains that humans emerged over millions of years from less advanced forms of life with God guiding the process.[5] As an evolutionary scientist, Teilhard held that evolution is a slow process of increasing complexity and that human beings emerge out of this slow evolutionary process.

To realize that humans are part of larger process that involves long spans of developmental time brings a massive change to all of our knowledge and beliefs. Teilhard did not see the human person as lost or insignificant because of evolution. Rather, he saw the human person as one truly unique, not a chance arrival but an integral element of the physical world. He described the distinct human in three ways: (1) The extreme physical-complexity (apparent in the brain size) marks the human person as the most highly synthesized form of matter known to us in the universe; (2) in light of this complexity, the human is the most perfectly and deeply centered of all cosmic particles within the field of our experience; and (3) the high degree of mental development (reflection, thought) places the human person above all other conscious beings known to us.[6] Thus, the human person is integrally part of evolution in that we rise from the process, but in reflecting on the process we stand apart from it. Teilhard defines reflection as "the power acquired by a consciousness to turn in upon itself, to take possession of itself *as an object* . . . no longer merely to know, but to know that one knows."[7] He quotes

---

[5] "The Latest Gallup Poll on Evolution" (2014), http://ncse.com/news/2014/06/latest-gallup-poll-evolution-0015653.

[6] Pierre Teilhard de Chardin, *The Future of Man*, trans. Norman Denny (New York: Harper and Row, 1964), 90.

[7] Teilhard de Chardin, *The Phenomenon of Man*, 165.

a phrase of Julian Huxley: the human person "is nothing else than evolution become conscious of itself." To this idea Teilhard adds, "The consciousness of each of us is evolution looking at itself and reflecting upon itself."[8] Thus the human person emerges from the evolutionary process and is integral to evolution. The person is "the point of emergence in nature, at which this deep cosmic evolution culminates and declares itself."[9] Evolution is the process by which life complexifies, emerging in the self-reflexive conscious human person.

Consciousness and Unity

Teilhard insisted that evolution is an ascent toward consciousness and is moving forward to a type of supreme consciousness, a noosphere (from the Greek *nous,* "mind") of coreflective thought and action. This may seem, prima facie, contrary to our highly individualized world, but, he insists, it is the nature of consciousness to center itself constantly upon everything and to be drawn to other centers of consciousness.[10] Evolution proceeds in the direction of hyperreflexion and thus hyper-personalization. One has only to take note today how the Internet, cell phone, and travel have given birth to global consciousness. "Are we not experiencing the first symptoms of an aggregation of a still higher order," Teilhard asks, "the birth of some single center from the convergent beams of millions of elementary centers [of consciousness] dispersed over the surface of the thinking earth?"[11] He goes on to say that because space-time contains and engenders consciousness, it is necessarily of a convergent nature. In other words, the multiple centers of consciousness are being drawn together and hypercentrated in Omega, despite the opposing forces of separation. These centers of consciousness, according to Teilhard, are our very selves and personalities

---

[8] Ibid., 221.

[9] Teilhard de Chardin, *Human Energy*, 23.

[10] Teilhard de Chardin, *The Phenomenon of Man,* 259.

[11] Ibid., 259.

grounded in Omega: "The very center of our consciousness, deeper than all its radii . . . is the essence which Omega, if it is to be truly Omega, must reclaim."[12]

If Omega is God and God is in evolution, then we cannot find ourselves by any other means than by centering ourselves in Omega in evolution: the universal must find itself in the particular and the particular must find itself in the universal. We cannot find our true identity, for example, by dispossessing ourselves of material things for the benefit of others, as if these will satisfy the pull of evolution toward more being and life. Rather, we must give our *entire self* to the other, as Teilhard wrote: "My ego must subsist [in Omega] through abandoning itself or the gift will fade away."[13] Evolution demands wholehearted involvement in a way consonant with the words of Jesus: "If you wish to be my disciple you must renounce yourself, take up your cross, and follow me" (Matt 16:24). While we may interpret the call to renunciation as self-denial, Jesus calls us to self-gift, immersing ourselves in the divine newness of love. For Teilhard, the gift of self in relation to Omega is movement toward a collective unity in love. He writes: "In any domain—whether it be the cells of a body, the members of a society or the elements of a spiritual synthesis—union differentiates. . . . The more 'other' they become in conjunction, the more they find themselves as 'self.'"[14] The paradox of Teilhard's thought is that trans-ego collective consciousness does not dissolve personhood but rather is the very basis of personhood. He writes: "The peak of ourselves, the acme of our originality, is not our individuality but our person; according to the evolutionary structure of the world, we can only find our person by uniting together."[15] He moves beyond the monastic (solitary) archetype to a new axial theology marked by collective consciousness. In the new age of evolution, self-introspection and/or the salvation of the individual are contrary to the evolutionary impulse toward

---

[12] Ibid., 261.
[13] Ibid., 261.
[14] Ibid., 262.
[15] Ibid., 263.

greater unity and love. Thus, he calls us to a new level of consciousness, beyond our individual souls toward a new collective
unity. "It is *beyond* our souls that we must look," he writes, "*not
the other way round.*"[16]

From Teilhard to Bruteau:
Evolutionary Personhood

Teilhard laid out a vision of evolution moving toward a fullness
of unity in love through the rise of human consciousness, and no
one understood his vision more profoundly than Beatrice Bruteau. In several seminal essays she explored a theology of personhood in light of energy, love, and consciousness. Her theology is
not conceptual but phenomenological and hence experiential and
praxis oriented, following the lines of Teilhard's Omega-centered
evolution. In her essay "The Living One," Bruteau seeks to move
beyond the Boethian notion of person as *persona est rationalis
naturae individua substantia* (a person is an individual substance
of a rational nature).[17] Building on the insights of quantum physics and trinitarian reality, she affirms that personhood begins
with relationality. The word *person* has the Latin root *sonare*
(literally, "to sound through") so that a person is one in whom
there is a sounding through *(per)* rather than an "individual substance." The notion of person arose in Christian thought from
the Greek Cappadocian Fathers and their understanding of the
Trinity as three communicable centers of shared life. The Greek
view of the Trinity emphasizes not so much the singular nature
of the Godhead as the intercommunion of the living persons.
Each person is so filled with the energy of self-giving to the others in outpouring love that a reciprocal iruption or unceasing
circulation of life results. This is the perichoresis of the Trinity,
whereby each person indwells the others and this interchange of

---

[16] Ibid., 260.

[17] The definition is given in Boethius's *Liber de Persona et duabus
naturis*, ch. 3. 2.

love and life is what produces or constitutes the divine unity.[18] If divine, perichoretic love is the source and flow of all being, then relationship is the *ontos* of being itself and community is the archetype.

Modern physics points to intrinsic relationality at the heart of life. The discovery of special relativity and the intercovertibility of mass and energy ($E = mc^2$) has impelled scientists to suggest that matter is not composed of building blocks but complicated webs of energy relations; interconnectedness lies at the core of all that exists. Bruteau speaks of a metaphysics of communion, and by this she means that relationship is the basic principle of life: God is relationship, matter is relationship, and human life is relationship, which means we need a new philosophical understanding of nature that begins with relationality. A metaphysics of communion based on intrinsic relationality undergirds a new understanding of the human person.

Is Individual and Person the Same?

Bruteau distinguishes between an individual and a person by saying that an "individual" is an individuated existent with a less-complexified consciousness of otherness, whereas a "person" is one who has a higher level of other-centered consciousness. An individual is in the first stage of reflexive consciousness, while personhood reflects a higher stage of self-reflexive consciousness. Hence, she indicates, only persons can enter into communion consciousness; individuals remain external to one another:

Evolution has produced reflexive consciousness. . . . Consciousness of ourselves from the outside was only a first stage of this reflexivity. . . . The evolutionary pressure toward greater reflexivity urges us to a realization of ourselves as conscious *of* being conscious, a noetic coincidence

---

[18] Beatrice Bruteau, "The Living One: Transcendent Freedom Creates the Future," in *The Grand Option: Personal Transformation and a New Creation* (Notre Dame, IN: University of Notre Dame Press, 2001), 143.

with ourselves as conscious acts of life-communicating life. This noetic coincidence with the act of communicating life is itself a free act; it is now our interior act that nevertheless enters more profoundly into the interiority of our *fellow* beings than ever an external act touched the exteriority of an *other* being.[19]

It is this transcendence of the person over the individual that makes possible the communion consciousness of the new creation in Christ.[20] Reality is being with another in a way that is open to more union and more being. Building on Teilhard's primacy of love-energy, Bruteau writes that a person is not an individuated being; rather, a person is the unbounded activity of freely projecting energies or what she calls "spondic" (a Greek word that means "libation") energy;[21] I do not exist in order that I may possess; rather, I exist in order that I may give of myself, for it is in giving that I am myself. This differentiated self-gift of personhood arises out of a deep center within where humanity is held by divinity in utter silence and freedom:

> It [spondic energy] is an outpouring that is an act of reverence, of worship. We experience it as a projection of personal, spiritual, self-existent energy towards and into other persons, and even towards the infrapersonal universe. We will to pour our own life, our own existence, into others that they may be and may be abundantly.[22]

Bruteau goes on to explain that spondic energy does not originate out of thought or will; it is not the *act* of an individual. Rather, it comes from a deep, transcendent center, the still point where we are held in being by the embrace of divine Love. It

---

[19] Bruteau, "Freedom: 'If Anyone Is in Christ, That Person Is a New Creation,'" in *The Grand Option*, 157.

[20] Bruteau, "Freedom," 161.

[21] Bruteau, "Persons in Communion," in *The Grand Option*, 52.

[22] Ibid., 52.

originates spontaneously, arising only from itself; spondic energy is always free. When we affirm another with our spondic energy, it is the personal being (of the other) that is being affirmed, the central selfhood or the "personal" Omega center, so to speak. To affirm another, we need not sanction the person's behavior, especially if it is hurtful or evil; we do not need even to like the person in the sense of personality or emotional attraction. "All these belong to the 'individual,'" Bruteau writes, "not to the 'person.' The person transcends the individual's qualities, and the person is spondic energy, fresh every moment, having no past, utterly spontaneous and capable of new manifestations."[23]

Jesus was truly a person because his unbounded, spondic energy of love radiated outward as he encountered others. His deep and profound "I am," expressing his Abba-oneness, radiated outward toward the other as "May you Be!" This deep relatedness, "I am, may you be," is a consciousness of interbeing arising from the very interiority of the beings united, from their presence in the midst of each other. It is not a relationship that can be mandated because it is based on intrinsic union and must be freely accepted. The very core of each person's being, each one's freedom, has enacted the giving and receiving that constitute the union: "I am insofar as I am in you." Hence Jesus says, "If you try to preserve your life you will lose it and if you lose your life for my sake [for the sake of divine love which is life itself] you will find it" (cf. Matt 16:25). To stay on the level of individualism or to desire aloneness defies the interpersonal basis of life. Relationality (and hence interbeing) is our most fundamental reality both on the quantum level of physical life and the higher levels of conscious human life.

---

[23] Ibid., 53–54. Bruteau indicates that an evolutionary understanding of transcendent personhood requires a whole new understanding of the person as subject. She writes: "We cannot *look at* or *talk about* a subject. To do so is to convert it into an object. We must rather *noetically coincide with* our self by experiencing our own existence interiorly" (51).

Freedom: The Core of Personhood

The clue to transcendent selfhood, according to Bruteau, is freedom. Actions are free when they are determined by the acting person as the agent of action and not by someone else or some juridical norm outside the person. Jesus exemplified a type of acting that was spondic in nature, that is, a free energy of spontaneous goodwill oriented toward another, even if it meant violating the sacred laws, such as healing the blind man or picking corn on the Sabbath. What motivated this spondic energy of good will? Bruteau points to the power of Omega at the core of his life. Jesus had a sense of deep personal unity with God, as he said, "The Father and I are one" (John 10:30). He lived from an inexhaustible center of divine love that empowered him to act freely in love; only transcendent selfhood can exercise creative freedom.[24] It is this "love-in-freedom" and "freedom-in-love" that undergirds the type of love called *agape* or the love of self-gift. Bruteau writes that "agape is an exercise of creative freedom and is future-oriented. It addresses itself to what does not yet exist. Agape is active; it bursts with energetic desire that there is more being."[25] Jesus's agapic love was more than a desire to help others; rather, it was a spontaneous bursting forth of love arising out of a deep, Omega-centered inner freedom.

The act of living as persons in communion means living from the center of spondic energy, whereby our act of living unites with another's act of living, and both go on to unite with a third, and so on. Spondic energy undergirds a living net of radiant energies whereby each center indwells every other center. To

---

[24] Bruteau, "The Living One," 133. Bruteau asks how we know when we are living on the psychological level or the spiritual level. She writes: "Full freedom and spirituality are reached when we originate and initiate acts of creative self-giving, without any passivity. Such acts are truly spontaneous, being done by us as their authors." She goes on to say that most of us resist freedom and creativity (133).

[25] Ibid., 132.

love another, Bruteau states, is a creative act.[26] We love another not as a static being but as the other is on the point of coming into existence. To love another, therefore, is to contribute to the creation of the other as *this* person and thus to co-create the universe, since the whole of the universe is emerging in *this* person.

Loving and living are co-joined in Bruteau's thought. It is often argued that we bring our past with us. Sometimes it is said that our past tells us who we are. But our past does not tell us who we are except in the sense of providing a context for our description. If we recount our past, then we should be aware that we are the ones who have made the past to be as it is. To be among the living is far greater than belonging to the past. "Why should we look backward to find the origin of our life?" Bruteau asks. "When Jesus was questioned by the Jews about his identity he said, 'Abraham is dead, and so too are the prophets but a greater than Abraham is *here*'" (John 8:53). We, the living, contain all that the past is and more because we live on the brink of the future. However, we are only among the living if the fountain of living water springs up out of our *heart*, from the very *center* of ourselves as living, that is, from the present moment, just as it gives itself forward into the future as an act of creative freedom projecting out of spondic energy. The act of living, therefore, is on the interface between the present and the future, not between the present and the past. To live, Bruteau indicates, is to create the future; spondic energy is poured out toward the future. Thus when we love someone, we do not love that person's past. The

---

[26] Bruteau's deep insights on evolutionary personhood flow from her profound insights on the God-world relationship. In her essay "Trinitarian Personhood" (in *The Grand Option*) she writes that "our 'I,' our personhood, is not a *product* of God's action, something left over after the action has ceased. Rather it *is* God's action in the very actuality of acting. 'We' are not a thing but an activity. This is why God's activity of ecstatically moving out to us is an act of coinciding with our activity, just as our union with God will be our ecstatically moving out to God as an act of coinciding with God's activity. . . . This activity which we are and which God is, is the act of creative freedom, of initiative, of self-originated self-giving" (75).

person to whom our agapic love, our spondic energy, is directed is the person who is coming into existence, who stands on the horizon of the future.[27]

Jesus and Transcendent Personhood

When we understand the human person as a center of spondic energy, one who is free in love, we can grasp the significance of Jesus as one who loved without reserve and spoke without fear. Truth flowed from his heart as he reached out to heal the leper (Matt 8:3) and accepted water from the woman at the well (John 4:7). In Jesus we see that spondic love-energy is the energy of wholemaking; it is interbeing energy that flows into conscious community. The life of Jesus shows us that community can emerge from nothing other than freedom in love. Bruteau writes that Jesus shares his own life substance and life energy with his friends under the guise of food. Table sharing is more than feeding, according to Bruteau. It is the way of becoming nourishment for one another, so that life may become more abundant together. Jesus gives himself as nourishment for life. This is his love for others, and it is a creative love, drawing the disciples into a collective consciousness of unity or church. Hence, Jesus exemplifies what Bruteau calls "transcendent personhood."

Transcendent personhood reflects a new axial consciousness, an ecological consciousness of belonging to a whole. It is an understanding of human personhood that, essentially, inverts the Plotinian "alone to the Alone" by understanding personhood as "union toward more union." Like Teilhard, Bruteau sees the journey toward unity as one that looks beyond the individual soul toward the cosmic whole because God-Omega is at the heart of evolutionary life. Transcendent personhood is grounded in a metaphysics of unity/community (unfolding along the evolutionary lines of complexity-consciousness) and challenges the prevailing domination paradigm of social relations. Bruteau

---

[27] Bruteau, "The Living One," 137.

writes that a hierarchical pattern of relationships is based on ontological differences and operates on principles of mutual negation: I am *not* you, and you are *not* me. This metaphysics of alienation treats the "other" as radically different from oneself, promoting a consciousness of the "stranger."[28] She draws an insightful comparison between the domination paradigm of social relations and a communion paradigm. The communion paradigm is a reciprocal relation of the enhancement of being. Unlike the domination paradigm in which the elements are outside one another, the communion paradigm sees beings as *in* one another. To be *in* a fellow being means that instead of denying one's attributes, activities, and values, one gives them or somehow puts them *into* the fellow being. This is what Jesus did by putting himself, under the guise of food, literally *into* his companions. His substance and energy, his attributes, activities, and values were assimilated by them, and he lived in them as their own attributes, activities and values, as his many sayings of indwelling indicate: "Whoever receives you receives me" (Matt 10:40); "whatever anyone does to my brother or sister is done to me" (Matt 25:20); the works I have done you shall also do" (John 14:12). Jesus reveals the empowering presence of Omega as the unitive center of community; thus, when we live from the center of Omega, we are free to be food for one another.

One could interpret this interbeing, communal relatedness along the lines of quantum entanglement, which is a phenomenon of physics based on interacting particles. Physicist Erwin Schrödinger said: "If two separated bodies, each by itself known maximally, enter a situation in which they influence each other, and separate again, then there occurs regularly that which I have just called *entanglement* of our knowledge of the two bodies."[29] Quantum entanglement is nonlocal interaction or unmediated

---

[28] Bruteau, "Freedom," 153.

[29] Erwin Schrödinger, "The Present Situation in Quantum Mechanics: A Translation of Schrödinger's Cat Paradox Paper," trans. John D. Trimmer, *Proceedings of the American Philosophical Society* 124. Available online.

action at a distance, without crossing space, without decay, and without delay.[30] David Bohm saw the phenomenon of quantum entanglement as undergirding an alternate view of reality. He interpreted the nonlocal effects as pointing to something new in reality that could not be attributed to causal connections. Bohm attributed the strange phenomenon of nonlocality to hidden variables or what he called the quantum potential, which complements Teilhard's Omega. Because of a principle of wholeness within reality, he spoke of a holomovement or implicate order as the basic understanding of reality.[31] Rather than starting with the parts and explaining the whole in terms of the parts, Bohm started with a notion of undivided wholeness and derived the parts as abstractions from the whole. Implicate order is a way of looking at reality not merely in terms of external interactions among things, but in terms of the internal (enfolded) relationships among things. "As human beings and societies we seem separate," he wrote, "but in our roots we are part of an indivisible whole and share in the same cosmic process."[32]

Bohm's term *holomovement* means that "movement" rather than "being" is primary. What may appear like permanent structures are only relatively autonomous sub-entities that emerge out of the whole of flowing movement and then dissolve back into it an unceasing process of becoming. Each relatively autonomous and stable structure ("relative" because each "part" is a whole and part of a larger whole) is understood not as an independent and permanent existent but as a product that has been formed in the whole flowing movement and that will ultimately dissolve back into this movement. How each whole-part forms and maintains itself depends on its place and function within the larger whole.[33]

[30] Arthur Fine, "The Einstein-Podolsky-Rosen Argument in Quantum Theory" (May 10, 2004; substantially revised Nov. 5, 2013), http://plato.stanford.edu/entries/qt-epr.

[31] Kevin J. Sharpe, "Relating the Physics and Metaphysics of David Bohm," http://www.ksharpe.com/Word/BM05.htm.

[32] David Bohm, *Wholeness and the Implicate Order* (New York: Routledge and Kegan Paul, 1980), 5.

[33] Sharpe, "Relating the Physics and Metaphysics of David Bohm."

Bruteau's communion paradigm finds a physical counterpart in Bohm's ideas on holomovement and implicate order. The unity attained by communion arises from the very interiority of the beings united from their presence in the midst of each other, and it must be freely accepted. Union is intrinsic. The very core of each person's being, each one's freedom, has enacted the giving and receiving that constitute the union: *I am* insofar as I am in you. The domination paradigm, on the other hand, is built on a metaphysics of alienation and rooted in a logic of self-identity by mutual negation—I am *not* you. The communion paradigm is based on a metaphysics of unity, rooted in a logic of self-identity by mutual affirmation. Thus, the secret of self-identity does not lie in an external set of boundaries of what I am and am not (the superficial layers of my existence) but in an internal coincidence of my Omega center with your Omega center in the act of living itself. This is the core of Teilhard's thought as well: "To communicate itself, my ego must subsist (exist in another) through abandoning itself or the gift will fade away," he wrote.[34] To live is to communicate life, because life is essentially an evolving phenomenon, a moving toward the future by moving toward greater complexity and consciousness. The more one affirms life in one's fellows and gives oneself to enhance their lives, the more one is truly alive and thus truly oneself.[35] Bruteau indicates that a communion paradigm of interrelatedness reflects the metaphysical shift needed to form a new ethics of life:

We have not had a metaphysics to sustain our morality. By metaphysics I mean . . . the way we see reality without thinking about it, our taken-for-granted perception of being, or outlook on life. Our morality tells us to love others as ourselves. But our metaphysics says that others are alien to ourselves. Others are outside us, different, in competition with us. . . . The basic recommendation for the good life is not to love your neighbor as much as you love yourself,

---

[34] Teilhard de Chardin, *The Phenomenon of Man*, 261.
[35] Bruteau, "Freedom," 156.

or even in the same way as you love yourself. It is to love your neighbor *as actually being yourself.* The fundamental perception of selfhood has to change before we can have the moral world we want.[36]

Faithful to the creative evolutionary vision of Teilhard, she indicates that our sense of self must change from the "dead" periphery of the personality description ("I am this and I am that") to a living core of transcendent and creative freedom ("I am, may you be!"). This is evolutionary thinking at its best. Eric Jantsch writes that "to live with an evolutionary spirit is to let go when the right time comes and to engage new structures of relationship."[37] Similarly, Bruteau writes that "to regard this 'instant' the moment to moment continuity of living—as the primary reality is essential to the future of life."[38] This new thinking requires us to relegate the past and the pseudo-future (the future of anxious anticipation) to the shadowy and unsubstantial secondary level of reality. A person is not the accumulation of the past, the spatialized substance that has some volume or weight to it, but the creative activity of life as it projects itself to the next instant. The person is not the product of the past but the process of the future. To be a person is to live in openness to the future because we are in evolution and thus in a process of becoming more whole and unified. Life eats through the shells of the dead, so to speak, and presses its way forward into the future.

Forgiveness: Creating a New Future

In a most insightful way Bruteau highlights the core gospel value of forgiveness as integral to evolution and weaves it into her Teilhardian scheme of evolutionary personhood. To be saved is

---

[36] Bruteau, "The Living One," 141.
[37] Eric Jantsch, *The Self-Organizing Universe* (Oxford: Pergamon Press, 1980), 1, 49.
[38] Bruteau, "The Living One," 142.

to be healed and made whole; forgiveness is the beginning of every new creative whole. Forgiveness is the gift of goodness given in abundance to another when love has been distorted or annihilated. The paradigm of forgiveness is the creative act of Jesus on the cross. Condemned to a wrongful death, innocent to the end, the crucified Jesus uttered the words of forgiveness from his dying lips: "Father, forgive them for they do not know what they do" (Luke 23:34). Out of his deep center of divine love Jesus returned goodness to his persecutors, who destroyed goodness by their actions. Thus, Jesus revealed his own inner freedom by freeing his persecutors to enter into a new future. To engage the present moment as a creative act, Bruteau indicates, requires a *consciousness* of forgiveness and reconciliation. If we relate only to the past deeds of others, we will always be at least one step behind where they themselves presently are and thus we will never really be in relationship with *them,* only with their "remains."[39] Rather, our act of living must be addressed to the other living person just at the point where that person is on the act of creating the next moment of life.

Bruteau sees forgiveness as having an essential role in the evolution of life; it is the act of loving another or giving over the good to another in the face of unresolved differences without trying to control the other. It is not a statement about the past; forgiveness is the act of making a new future because it the essence of love in general, the energetic radiation of a good will for the sake of the future. Jesus said: "Follow me and let the dead bury their own dead" (Matt 8:22), that is, you are to walk with me into a new life. This "giving forward" toward the future is the projection of spondic energy; forgiveness is an act of creative freedom and radical novelty. It is creative because where there is nothing left between disputing parties, forgiveness calls us to give out of an abundance of spondic love for the sake of a new future. Our well-wishing, our intention to give life and give it abundantly, unites with the other's creative act of stepping forward into the

---

[39] Ibid., 129.

next moment. Our affirmation is directed from our central self, the self that is transcendent and spondic, toward the other's transcendent and spondic self. Our spondic energy, therefore, is directed toward the future, for the good of the future. Hence, we give without constraints to go forward into the future for the sake of the future, a future unknown but open to a freedom of creativity. In doing so, we participate in the divine act of creating *ex nihilo*, out of nothing. In the spirit of forgiveness, we become co-creators of an evolving universe.

If Jesus's forgiveness is the act of making a new future, the resurrection of Jesus speaks to us of new life. We see in Jesus that death is not the end; our bodies do not become dust while the soul goes to heaven. Quantum physics helps us realize that death is the collapse of our "particle" aspect of life into the "wave" dimension of our relatedness.[40] While I am alive, I am changing and growing from one moment to the next. This is true of both my body and my character; indeed, of the whole pattern that is "me." The "I" that exists now, though woven in part from the cloth that was "me" yesterday, is an evolved person in whom yesterday's "I" is sublated into the new "I" of the present moment. I am always investing my future in another. While I am alive that other is "me"—my many selves that I am becoming; after I am dead, that other is you, because my own self is woven into yours. The process of my becoming continues. We live on in our relationships, and in and through our relationships, we are continuously created.[41]

This living on in and through relationships undergirds the resurrection of Jesus, an event without eyewitnesses but recounted by those who experienced Jesus in a new way after his death: on the road to Emmaus; in the breaking of the bread; on the shore of Lake Tiberias; and behind locked doors, where the human

---

[40] Ilia Delio, *Making All Things New: Catholicity, Cosmology, Consciousness* (Maryknoll, NY: Orbis Books, 2015), 84.

[41] Danah Zohar, *The Quantum Self: Human Nature and Consciousness Defined by the New Physics* (New York: Quill/William Morrow, 1990), 150–51.

finger of Thomas touched the wounds of Christ (John 20:27). Jesus lives on in the heart of the universe in a new relatedness; his death was not the end but the beginning of new life in God. Resurrection means that we too will live on to the extent that we live now; that is, to the extent that we focus our passion, loyalty, and care to family, friends, community, nation, to transcend ourselves in love. The magnitude of our relatedness is the breadth of our lives and the degree to which we live on in the evolution of life. To live eternal life is to live in the *now* unconditionally and wholeheartedly; to lose ourselves in love for the sake of new life.

The resurrection of Jesus Christ anticipates the destiny of the cosmos—a new field of cosmotheandric love permeating the cosmos.[42] The resurrection happens in the present moment, but it is a present moment bathed in future, a new relationship with God, a new union by which life becomes more whole, more unified and open to new life. Resurrection expresses the core of revelation: to be alive is to be constantly in the process of becoming a new creation, open to and resting on the future. Life is ever renewing itself; to be alive is to be ceaselessly beginning. This is the good news of revelation in Jesus: God is ever new, and when we are united to God we become new again.

Christ, the Living One

Evolutionary personhood, according to Bruteau, draws its life from Christ, the Living One. Jesus is the exemplar of relationality, the one in whom spondic energy radiates outward in the evolution of a new cosmic community centered in God. Two questions, in particular, occupy her thought. The first is the question of Jesus to his disciples: "Who do people say that I am?" (Mark 8:27). The second question is Pauline in nature: "What

---

[42] The term *theandric* was coined by Maximus the Confessor and refers to the union of divine and created energies. See Lars Thunberg, *Man and His Cosmos: The Vision of Saint Maximus the Confessor* (Crestwood, NY: St. Vladimir's Press, 1985); Andrew Louth, *Maximus the Confessor* (New York: Routledge, 1996).

does it mean to live 'in Christ'?" We need a shift in consciousness, she indicates, to produce the new creation that Paul describes as being "in Christ" (cf. Gal 3:27). For Bruteau, this shift in consciousness is a transition from a paradigm of domination to one of communion, from negation (I am not you) to being rooted in the unlimited activity of living itself (I am, may you be). The evolution of the new creation "in Christ" is a communion event: If anyone is in Christ, that person is a new creation; that is, if *we* are in Christ, *our* communion is a new creation. The type of communion Bruteau envisions is a community of co-reflective centers of consciousness, each of whom "in Christ" forms the body of Christ; it is a union of our deepest personal energies. Bruteau interprets the meaning of "in Christ" as transcendent personhood in evolution. By sharing love-energy and directing our good to another, we both participate in and co-create the hyper-personalizing universe, as Teilhard describes it. Christ emerges out of reconciling relationships of love where mind and heart are increasingly unified in shared vision and consciousness; that is, love gives birth to God all along the way of evolution, as life proceeds toward higher consciousness and union in love.

The gospel message is about life. Anything else, according to Bruteau, misses the vision of God, who is Life itself. To hope that we are going to "arrive" at some final destination or "attain" some type of world utopia distorts the message of Jesus. In a small essay entitled "Saving Jesus" Bruteau wrote: "The abundant universal unconditional graciousness goodness givingness of our warmly personal God is our central reality, our root, and it's secure. . . . You can realize it directly for yourself; you just have to pay deep attention to your own act of existing."[43] To be "in Christ" is to be in the dynamic flow of becoming, because the Messianic age is always coming.[44] It is *always* relative to whatever age we are now in. Life constantly seeks to renew itself and thus to transcend itself because the Christ is *always* the One

---

[43] Beatrice Bruteau, "Saving Jesus," *Radical Grace* (July-August-September 2007): 6.

[44] Bruteau, "Freedom," 167.

who is coming. Thus, every age must look forward to the coming of its Messiah, the One who will make all things new. Every age needs to be saved from the deadness of the forms it outgrows over time and to be lifted into a new kind of life. Whenever a new creation takes place, it takes place "in Christ."

The New Creation will always be both one and many, both unity and multiplicity, being generated by the same act of divine trinitarian love, the act of projecting life-giving energies toward fellow members of the community, that is, by agapic love. In the evolution of life each member is always itself a whole, and out of the fullness and intensity of one's own sense of wholeness there is a radiation of life-energy toward one's fellow persons. Each member uniquely contributes to the whole, and thus each member is absolutely indispensable to the emerging new level of wholeness. As the many are drawn into greater unity through a rise in consciousness and love, God emerges as transcendent oneness, the center of love and the unity of personhood. Divine love incarnate—in each one of us—*is* the Christ, and this Christ is inexhaustible in the dynamism of ever-converging fullness. When we are "in Christ" and realize ourselves as the "I am" whose life consists of saying to all "May you be," we are active members of this creative activity that makes all things new at every moment. Christ, the Living One, is found on the edge of tomorrow, participating in the creation of the coming day, for the Living One is also the Creating One. To live in a Christic universe means that life is always thrusting itself into the future. *We* are the New Creation in the active sense of being those who are participants in the act of creating.[45] By entering into Christ, we attain a new level of reflexivity; not only the consciousness of consciousness, the self-thinking thought, but the self-creating creature. Bruteau writes that "if we really accept creation as ever new, and if we ourselves are active participants in this ever new creating, then we are always facing the future."[46] We must not seek the Living One among the dead, that is, the past; the Living

---

[45] Ibid., 171.
[46] Ibid., 171.

One is not found there. Rather, the Living One is the One engaged in creating anew, evolving the new creation.

Teilhard spoke of Christogenesis as moving toward Omega or the fullness of Christ. Bruteau's transcendent personhood helps us understand more profoundly that Christ Omega *is* already within, evolution as its dynamic power. If the goal (the *pleroma* of Christ) is already within then we are not going toward a goal, as in arriving at a place (such as heaven); rather, we are discovering the goal that is our potentiality and capacity for divinity. To evolve into God is to evolve into the personal embrace of life itself; the goal *is* the journey. In this respect transcendence may be the most apt description of nature. We evolve to never stop evolving; life ceaselessly begins anew because God is ever newness in love. Bruteau writes that "creativity may be seen as the real interior meaning of the act of faith."[47] The Living One who is the creating and forgiving One is always *in* the act of faith in the future; or as Teilhard indicated, faith in God *is* faith in the future. Real creativity, therefore, arises originally and spontaneously from the heart of the agent, as from a first source, when one is Omega-centered. The act of faith is the act of uniting with the Living One as living, not dead, not bound by the past, but as transcendent, free, and creating. Faith is not an act of knowledge, "for knowledge is always of the past," Bruteau writes.[48] Rather, faith is an act of the imagination and trust in the future. To have faith is to enter into the other's creating, into the other's future, which has not yet appeared.

Bruteau brings together these deep insights on Christ the Living One and evolutionary personhood in a poetic, rhetorical refrain that concludes her essay on transcendent freedom:

> To enter by our transcendent freedom into Christ and to become a New Creation means to enter by faith into the future of every person and into the very heart of creativity itself, into the future of God. . . .

---

[47] Ibid., 172.
[48] Ibid., 172.

To be "in Christ" is to accept the offer that Jesus makes, to be food for his friends. . . .

To be "in Christ" is to abandon thinking of oneself only in terms of categories and abstractions by which one may be externally related to others and to coincide with oneself as a transcendent center of energy that lives *in* God and *in* one's fellows—because that is where the Christ lives, in God and in us.

To be "in Christ" is to experience oneself as an initiative of free energy radiating out to give life abundantly to all, for that is the function of the Christ. . . .

To be "in Christ" is to be identified with the Living One who is not to be sought among the dead, for the Living One is the One who is Coming to Be.[49]

In Bruteau's evolutionary paradigm the human person is co-creative of the future. The human person is the one who lives in God and consciously participates in the evolution of God, the divine center of unity and love. The significance of the humanity of Jesus is our humanity: "Christ has no body on earth but yours," according to the Teresian prayer. Hence, what we become as human persons has an impact on the Christ; how we choose to act for the future shapes the future coming of Christ. Christ is not a principle but the divine gift of relational life, the trinitarian *holos*, revealed in Jesus and brought to the fullness of life in and through us. What Bruteau points out is that God enters into our world when Christ is born within us; we *are* the mothers of Christ, the birthgivers, and thus it matters to God—literally—what we become. She concludes her essay on transcendent freedom in a lyrical vision of Christogenesis:

If I am asked, then, "Who do you say I am?" my answer is: "You are the new and ever renewing act of creation. You are all of us, as we are united in You. You are all of us as we live in one another. You are all of us in the whole

---

[49] Ibid., 172–73.

cosmos as we join in Your exuberant act of creation. You are the Living One who improvises at the frontier of the future; and it has not yet appeared what You shall be.[50]

Conclusion

Although Teilhard had a deep vision of the cosmos and Christ evolving into unity, Bruteau offered a keen analysis of the next steps toward a hyper-personalizing Christic universe. She brings together evolution, Christogenesis, and self-reflective personhood in a sweeping vision of the cosmic Christ as the personalizing center of the evolving universe. Like Teilhard, she believes it is not something but *Someone* who is in evolution. That *Someone* includes each one of us—the Christic dimension of our lives— but to realize this Christic dimension we must shed the old coat of Greek metaphysics undergirding our individual souls and awaken to our deepest center within, which is Omega, uniting on a higher level of consciousness and love. Evolution, as Bruteau realized, calls for a whole new "location" of our selfhood, and this is nothing short of a revolution in consciousness. It is the consciousness of belonging, mutual affirmation, participation, and creative love by which each one gives of one's life to foster life in others; a type of consciousness that perceives existentially rather than essentially. It is a consciousness of shared values and shared goodness, a consciousness of belonging together and sharing a future together. She spoke of conversion to this integral level of consciousness by nurturing the uniqueness of individuals as participants in a cosmic whole: "The more conscious the individual becomes, the more individual becomes *person*, and each person is person only to the extent that the individual freely lives by the life of the Whole."[51] Conversion is the root

---

[50] Ibid., 173.
[51] Beatrice Bruteau, "The Whole World: A Convergent Perspective," in *The Grand Option*, 102.

of inner freedom by which one creatively participates as person in the evolution of self and world: "The evolution of personal consciousness becomes thus a spiral of convergence, activated by delight in creating the future."[52]

I imagine that if Teilhard and Beatrice were standing on the deck of a space ship traveling into the future, Teilhard would be in awe at the vastness and wonder of the cosmos, while Beatrice would suggest to him how the next level of planet evolution will unfold, through transcendent personhood. Teilhard would turn and say to her, "Mais Oui! We shall call this next level of co-reflective consciousness the 'ultra-human.'" And Beatrice would agree that a higher level of ultra-human consciousness undergirds the emergence of Christ the Living One. For Teilhard and Bruteau, the mystery of divine love is disclosed in evolution as the ceaseless exploration of life toward the fullness of life. Nature is never satisfied with itself; it always presses on to be more, and it presses for novelty. When we participate in this drive for new possibilities, we participate also in God; self-transcendence itself *is* ultimate reality.[53]

Bruteau maintains that personhood, transcendence, and creative freedom are "the real interior meaning of the act of faith."[54] It is not a matter of "doing this" or "following that"; rather, it is a matter of living and of creating the future. Forgiveness plays an essential role in getting us out of the ruts of sameness or deadness because the essence of forgiveness is the essence of love in general, "the energetic radiation of a good will for the sake of the future."[55] Jesus, the Forgiving One, dwells in the midst of fragile living beings, where the rescuing and healing and further creating continue amid life's struggles; where imagination, novelty, caring, sharing, and enjoying are found; where life continues to find itself on new levels of consciousness and creativity, never

---

[52] Ibid., 102.

[53] Philip Hefner, *Technology and Human Becoming* (Minneapolis: Fortress Press, 2003), 85.

[54] Bruteau, "Freedom," 172.

[55] Bruteau, "The Living One," 129.

stopping or ceasing in its striving to be fully alive. Christ *is* the Living One, life unto life, glory unto glory, the future of life itself, and what the fullness of Christ Omega will be is yet to be seen.

7

Teilhard de Chardin
and the Millennial Milieu

BRIE STONER

*At this very moment we have reached a delicate point
of balance at which a readjustment is essential. It could
not, in fact, be otherwise: our Christology is still expressed in exactly the same terms as those which, three
centuries ago, could satisfy men whose outlook on the
cosmos it is now physically impossible for us to accept.*
—TEILHARD DE CHARDIN,
Christianity and Evolution

Whenever I go to a spiritual retreat or a contemplative conference I am usually cornered in a matter of hours. Someone, at
some point, will inevitably ask, "Do you mind me asking how
old you are? And how exactly did you come to be here?" Never
mind the ego catnip of such well-intentioned curiosity by which I
get to feel both special *and* young but, at 32, it is true, I am usually one among a numbered few at contemplative events whose
hair isn't peppered with gray. Likewise, when visiting churches
there is usually an extra-enthusiastic dose of welcoming, while
among my peers I am among a small minority of people who

consider themselves practicing Christians. I say "visiting" because, as hard as I have tried to find a church home in the last ten years, I cannot escape the feeling haunting most of my generation: we are spiritual orphan misfits. Since discovering the work of Teilhard de Chardin, however, I have begun to wonder if our collective generational frustration with religion isn't the sign of a new evolution in humanity. Perhaps we have sprouted spiritual wings, yet still crawl around on our bellies trying to be caterpillars, unable to figure out why going to church feels "off."

According to a 2014 Pew Research study, the millennial generation—those born between 1978 and 2000—are much less inclined to self-identify as religious,[1] while another study demonstrated that three out of four millennials identified as "spiritual but not religious."[2] The Pew Center followed this study with a published report in 2015 titled "America's Changing Religious Landscape," detailing how Christianity is on the decline while the affiliation of religious "nones" has grown from 16.1 percent to 22.8 percent in the last seven years.[3] Religious "nones," largely the rising cohort of millennials reaching adulthood, demonstrate what has become self-evident by the empty pews of Christian churches across the United States: church isn't working for the majority of the next generation.

A 2011 Barna research study showed that no one reason was found to be dominant in explaining why the earliest millennials have begun an exodus away from the church.[4] Instead, researchers in another study discovered six major themes for why three

---

[1] Paul Taylor, Carroll Doherty, Kim Parker, and Vidya Krishnamurthy, "Millennials in Adulthood" (Washington, DC: Pew Research Center, March 7, 2014).

[2] Thom S. Rainer and Jess W. Rainer, *The Millennials* (Nashville, TN: B&H Publishing, 2011), 22.

[3] Alan Cooperman, Gregory Smith, Kathering Ritchey, "America's Changing Religious Landscape" (Washington, DC: Pew Research Center, May 12, 2015).

[4] The 2011 study is included in David Kinnaman and Aly Hawkins, *You Lost Me: Why Young Christians Are Leaving the Church and Rethinking Church* (Grand Rapids, MI: Baker Books Publishing, 2011).

out of every five young Christians (59 percent) were leaving the church.[5] Among them were "the church is stifling . . . fear-based (23 percent) and ignoring the problems of the real world (22 percent)"; "Christianity is shallow, boring (31 percent) and not relevant to my interests (24 percent)"; "the church is antagonistic to science, with three out of ten saying that church is out of step with the scientific world we live in (29 percent)"; and "Christianity is too exclusive, with three out of ten citing that churches are afraid of the beliefs of other faiths (29 percent)." Kinnaman concludes that these challenges to Christianity should be addressed in what he proposes as the median approach of building intergenerational relationships rather than catering to the next generation, which, in his words, "builds the church on the preferences of young people and not on the pursuit of God." Although the idea of intergenerational relationships and building "the body of Christ" is not against the grain of millennial network thinking, when such relationships are created with the sole intent of forming a net to keep millennials in narrow and exclusive belief systems, it is missing the glaring point made evident by the results of the research.

With such a well-educated and diverse generation,[6] and a global interconnectivity in which networking is replacing institution, to subscribe to the narrow belief systems of organized religion requires the denial of one's education in science or the condemnation of others' sexual preferences or is simply antipodal to the general growing collective consciousness. Likewise, participating in a religion that paints humans as essentially unworthy recipients of individual salvation from a material world that must be denied and rejected is incongruous with the millennial optimistic creative impetus, social activism, and environmental concern.[7] Christianity, in its current esoteric iteration, has all but lost its value in the face of the millennial generation,

---

[5] "Six Reasons Young Christians Leave Church" (Ventura, CA: Barna Group, September 28, 2011).

[6] Pew Research Center, "Millennials in Adulthood."

[7] David D. Burstein, *Fast Future* (Boston: Beacon Press, 2013), 3.

which is more concerned with the quality of the interior fruit and the process of its transformation than the institutional church's obsession over the shape of the wineskin.

In my case, the disillusionment with the church and my exodus from religious institutions that followed was not driven by rebellion, but rather by an intuition—an inner compass that pulled me like a magnet away from what had become a constrictive, narrow, and exclusive belief system and toward the promise of a more spacious spiritual expanse, one capable of being as dynamically inclusive as the universe itself. Without much context or guidance for how to categorize this deep intuition, I, like many in my generation, have had little choice but to shed the held membership in institutional religion and join the masses of my "spiritual but not religious" cohort. Through the writings of the Christian mystics I began to comprehend this exodus as part of the Christian mystical formation, in which one begins to learn how to hold paradox in creative tension, allowing a more inclusive, non-dual consciousness to emerge. It was the voice of one lone mystic in particular, however, that spoke not only to my personal journey but to the collective *whole* philosophical shift evinced by my generation, placing these changes in a greater context. This voice belongs to French paleontologist and priest Pierre Teilhard de Chardin.

A New Lens for a New Age

Teilhard de Chardin provides a new lens by which to view the unfolding story of humanity. His is an evolutionary perspective in which, at long last, we might begin to comprehend humanity *not* as the fallen dense matter incapable of divine relationship without an intermediary atonement, but as uniquely and necessarily part of the great differentiated union of God's expressed love in the unfolding story of creation. Through Teilhard's evolutionary frame, matter and spirit can finally cease their dualistic battle, which has been foundational to the first axial religions, by shifting our frustrated ontology of *being* into an evolutionary ontology of *becoming*. In Teilhard's words, "Nothing can any longer find place in our constructions which does not first satisfy the conditions of a universe in process of transformation."[8] Like a prophet in the wilderness, Teilhard's archeological studies in the far reaches of the Chinese deserts led him to comprehend a greater cosmic unfolding narrative, thereby making him capable of anticipating the signs of the transition taking place in our time as the necessary unfolding evolution into Christ-Omega.

While older generations decry the lack of apparent religious interest or devotion displayed by millennials, it is my premise that the root issue underlying this alleged spiritual ambivalence lies with the entrenchment of our religious traditions in static and outdated dogma and the insistence on maintaining the church as a localized institution, *not* the spiritual capacity of the next generation. I echo Teilhard in his observations that our current lack of religious interest demonstrates the failure of religion to animate the human spirit:

> We are surrounded by a certain sort of pessimist who con-tinually tells us that our world is foundering in atheism. But should we not rather say that what it is suffering from is *unsatisfied theism?* Men, you say, no longer want God; but are you quite sure that what they are rejecting is not simply the image of a God who is too insignificant to nourish in us this concern to survive and super-live to which the need to worship may ultimately be reduced?[9]

The rise of the feminine is an apt metaphor for the dawning of an age that promises the birthing of new ideologies capable of nurturing and fostering the growth of the collective human body. In an evolutionary framework each generation is the ideological

---

[8] Pierre Teilhard de Chardin, *Christianity and Evolution*, trans. René Hague (New York: Harcourt, 1971), 78.

[9] Pierre Teilhard de Chardin, *Activation of Energy*, trans. René Hague (London: Williams Collins Sons, 1978), 239–40.

progeny of the previous generations' conscious labor. Through the theology of visionaries such as Pierre Teilhard de Chardin and Beatrice Bruteau, new luminous spiritual possibilities have slowly and steadily been forming in the dark womb of the collective unconscious, not yet ready to manifest their full potential. It is my belief that the age of the millennials is the fruition of this spiritual conception, a generation already demonstrating the characteristics that evince the very advent of a new evolutionary species capable of operating from a cosmic whole that Teilhard described as "ultra-humanity."

I seek to present how the evolutionary framework of Teilhard de Chardin provides the necessary key to untangle much of what is seemingly irreconcilable between millennials and Christian theology by addressing three critical aspects to Christian dogma that require a "system update" in order to become compatible with the future of humanity. In his essay "Christianity and Evolution: Suggestions for a New Theology," Teilhard underscores this critical transition:

> In the first century of the Church, Christianity made its definitive entry into human thought by boldly identifying the Christ of the gospel with the Alexandrian Logos. The logical continuation of the same tactics and the prelude to the same success must be found in the instinct which is now urging the faithful, after two thousand years, to return to the same policy; but this time it must not be with the ordinating principle of the stable Greek kosmos but with the neo-Logos of modern philosophy—the evolutive principle of a universe in movement.[10]

Teilhard outlines the orthodoxy that has become incompatible with the seeds of a burgeoning global humanity in his essay "Christology and Evolution," which I loosely condense here under three subjects: (1) "Evolution and the Past," (2) "Evolution

---

[10] Teilhard de Chardin, *Christianity and Evolution,* 181.

and the Present," and (3) "Evolution and the Future." These three aspects of Teilhard's theological contribution address the critical areas of Christology that otherwise conflict with the growing millennial milieu, characterized by its education, global inclusivity, and pragmatic idealism.

Evolution and the Past

If you were to ask someone to sum up the Christian narrative, you would be likely to hear the familiar story of how Adam and Eve "sinned" in the garden; how because of that we are all "sinners"; and that the only way to remedy our "sinfulness" is by professing belief in Jesus Christ as our intermediary, and then trying to be "good." If you were to ask a millennial the same question, you would be likely to hear the same story, but perhaps with additionally exaggerated quotation gestures around "sin" that underscore the collective frustration with viewing our humanity as "unworthy" or "fallen." The reticence to subscribe to the duality of the first axial religious construct demonstrates the collective intuition that the problem of evil is more complex than simply pinning it on Adam, one member of humanity, let alone pinning it blindly onto the entire human family. In order to understand the millennial discomfort with viewing humanity as "unworthy," we must begin our exploration with the dissonance between an evolutionary framework and the Christian narrative.

Back to the Future

The crux of the Christian story has thus far been resting on the past, beginning with a view that humanity's transgressions caused a "fall" from a perfectly completed creation, a "foundational" past that is incongruent with what we know scientifically about our human lineage. We must go back and examine the ground of how we conceive of our human origins, for it is how we think of our past that shapes the potential of our future. Up until now the Christian, seeking to be faithful to the tradition, has had to develop a split personality; on the one hand believing that the tradition had something of great spiritual value despite its seeming contradiction with science, and on the other a concession to the discovery of evolution, despite its contradiction with the story of creation upon which Christology hinges. Teilhard addresses original sin as the first and largest hurdle to an evolutionary theology in this work:

> Whenever we try intellectually and vitally to assimilate Christianity with all our modern soul, the first obstacles we meet always derive from original sin. . . . Original sin, in its present representation, is a constant bar to the natural development of our religion. It clips the wings of hope: we are incessantly eager to launch out into the wide open field of conquest which optimism suggests, and every time it drags us back inexorably into the *overpowering* darkness of reparation and expiation.[11]

Teilhard describes original sin and the story of fallen creation as a "static solution to the problem of evil."[12] In a fully formed world that issued from the Creator's hands in a completed state, there is no accounting for evil and suffering except through a "secondary distortion," a corruption of some sort: a charming snake and a forbidden apple, for example. Therefore, Teilhard continues, most of our theology has been formed resting on the foundation that "all the evil around us was born from an initial transgression. So far as dogma is concerned, we are still living in the atmosphere of a universe in which what matters most is reparation and expiation."[13] The static universe demands the righting of the scales in order to make sense of death and suffering. However, in an evolutive paradigm the universe is not complete; rather, it is still in the act of becoming, and as such we

---

[11] Ibid., 80.
[12] Ibid.
[13] Ibid., 81.

must assign God's omnipotence not to an instantaneous creation but to the continued process of uniting:

> Pure act and "non-being" are diametrically opposed in the same way as are perfected unity and pure multiple. This means that in spite of (or rather because of) his perfections, the Creator cannot communicate himself immediately to his creature, but must make the creature capable of receiving him. If God is to give himself to the plural, he must unify it to his own measure.[14]

In an evolutionary framework, where God as Creator cannot create except evolutively, the problem of evil and the function of free will are synthesized by way of a dynamic *hyper*physics:[15] evolution in the process of *uniting rather than a static ontology of being*. The universe did not appear fully formed, implying that the work of creation and creating is somehow finished and complete, but rather all of life is in the continual process of creating and evolving and is in fact not finished. In the ecstatic expression of God-Creator poured out into material multiplicity, which is slowly and over deep time capable of converging upon greater union and complexity, we find the grounds for the "manifest and mysterious association between matter and spirit."[16] In such a paradigm evil is the

> inevitable chance . . . which accompanies the existence of all participated being. Wherever being *in fieri* [in process of becoming] is produced, suffering and wrong immediately appear as its shadow: not only as a result of the tendency towards inaction and selfishness found in creatures but also . . . as the inevitable concomitant of their effort to

---

[14] Ibid., 83.

[15] Ilia Delio, *The Unbearable Wholeness of Being* (Maryknoll, NY: Orbis Books, 2013), 45–46.

[16] Teilhard de Chardin, *Christianity and Evolution*, 179.

progress. Original sin is the essential reaction of the finite to the creative act.[17]

In other words, sin and suffering are part of the package of how evolution works. Sin is not a problem to be eradicated; it is simply the counterstroke of life itself in the process of becoming more complex, more organized, and *more unified*.

A House Built on Rock

Just like Jesus's parable of the two builders, the foundation of how we understand our origins is critical in determining our capacity to live into our potential as the body of Christ. Thus far the Christian narrative has been resting on "shifting sand" in light of what we now know to be true of our evolutionary origins. Therefore, a transition off such substratum is critical in order to preserve the edifice of our faith from collapsing into incoherence.

A synthesis of this nature between evolution and theology would not only create a harmonic resonance between the next generation of Christian millennials and modern science, but it would also begin to release the weight of collective shame carried by humanity with the religious perpetuation of the doctrine of original sin. Little can be accomplished in this world if humanity's impetus is cut off at the knees by the weight of guilt and a sense of unworthiness that will only further perpetuate antiquated psychologies and spiritual impotence. Instead, the story of creation gains luminous optimism when we shift away from a static universe to an unfinished universe still in the act of becoming; evolution happens through the continued arrangement and synthesis into union of what was once a disorganized multiplicity.[18] This transition in our dogma from an instantaneous creation to creation through evolution, and from original sin to understanding sin as original *states*, would correlate with the spirit of creativity and entrepreneurship that the modern human spirit is so fluent

---

[17] Ibid., 40.
[18] Ibid., 178.

in. This is an endeavor that the millennial generation, noted as the most entrepreneurial in history,[19] understands and can make sense of. We know in the marrow of our bones that to create *is* to risk and that it entails pain, frustration, and suffering.

> New being, launched into existence and not yet completely assimilated into unity, is a dangerous thing, bringing with it pain and oddity. For the Almighty, therefore, to create is no small matter: it is no picnic, but an adventure, a risk, a battle to which he commits himself unreservedly. Can we not see what breadth and clarity is beginning to be added to the mystery of the Cross?[20]

For Teilhard, the original state of disorder and sin is the cost of evolution; an essential part of the universe all along, not a corruption of paradise incurred by an individual's actions in a garden. Suffering is the painful byproduct of a universe in motion, the price of an ecstatic creation infused with free will on its progressive groping path toward more complex unified being. It is the "shadow" of the creative act and a much more compelling context for the Incarnation than merely reparation: God becoming united in the course of evolution, demonstrating the way forward to an ultimate evolutionary convergence of consciousness and love.

Evolution and the Present

As the millennials crest into adulthood and flood the marketplace, the comfort in our diverse ranks and the growing proclivity toward identifying as "planetary" rather than "national" is becoming more apparent by our generation's willingness to enter into intra-spiritual dialogues and practices. In such a growing global atmosphere the imperialistic overtones toward

---

[19] Burstein, *Fast Future*, 96.
[20] Teilhard de Chardin, *Christianity and Evolution*, 84–85.

"conquering" other faiths through evangelism and conversion are dissonant in relation to the cosmic dimensions of Christ, which Teilhard asserts is the missing dimension in our Christology.

Christ, the Evolver

Teilhard declares our emphasis in Christology has thus far considered the Man-Jesus and the Word-God but failed to highlight the "Christ of the eucharist, and the parousia, the cosmic, consummating Christ of St. Paul."[21] This third, cosmic nature of Christ is a key theological contribution that Teilhard sought to reveal, that of the Universal Christ. The Incarnate Christ, as Teilhard postulated, "inoculates" matter with the capacity of continuing the course of the divine arc into union with Christ, or as theologian Raimon Panikkar describes it in the title of his work, it is the continual *Christophany*. The event of the incarnation didn't just happen as a singular event; it is *happening* even now, catalyzed by that singular event.

> A nonreductive Christian vision should be able to assert that every being is a Christophany, a manifestation of the Christic adventure of the whole of reality on its way to infinite mystery. I repeat, the whole of reality could be called, in Christian language, Father, Christ, Holy Spirit— the Font of all reality, reality in its act of being (that is, its becoming, the existing reality which is "the whole Christ" (Christus totus), not yet fully realized, and the Spirit (the wind, the divine energy that maintains the perichoresis in movement).[22]

Panikkar believes that our Christology has lost its mystical foundation because it lacks what he calls a "cosmovision" (a theology that includes cosmology), leaving our theology vulnerable to becoming "empty talk or being misunderstood." Modern

---

[21] Ibid., 179.
[22] Raimon Panikkar, *Christophany* (Maryknoll, NY: Orbis Books, 2004), 146.

Christology, Panikkar says, needs the third, missing mystical dimension in order for this dynamism to exist. We have forgotten that *Christ* was not Jesus's last name, but rather a messianic term he was anointed with, a mystery great enough for all of humanity to participate in and described by the apostle Paul as forming the "body" of Christ.[23]

Jesus was indeed the Christ, but the Christ is not limited to the person of Jesus. The historical Jesus of Nazareth personalizes by his life, death, and resurrection what is cosmically incarnationally true: the direction of Love is toward unification, always resulting in new and more abundant life. Therefore, we can now understand the Cosmic Christ as Christ, the evolver. Teilhard writes:

> If we are to effect the synthesis between faith in God and faith in the world, for which our generation is waiting, there is nothing better we can do than dogmatically to bring out, in the person of Christ, the cosmic aspect and function which make him organically the prime mover and controller, the "soul" of evolution.[24]

To this Christ the modern age of humanity can bring its true worship, for it is a Christ that fills the cosmic dimensions of space and time and, as such, not only permits but *requires* us to evolutively shed all ideologies that further exclusion and condemnation that diminish Christ. In such a perspective Christ becomes the *catalyst* of *all* evolution as the animating presence to which each individual responds in an evolution hinged on our participation, the personal heartbeat behind all progress and awakening consciousness. "Cosmogenesis" becomes "Christogenesis,"[25] not in a disembodied ideology, but in a deeply intimate and mystically incarnate reality. What is awakening in our collective

---

[23] Ilia Delio, *Christ in Evolution* (Maryknoll, NY: Orbis Books, 2008), 33.

[24] Teilhard de Chardin, *Christianity and Evolution*, 180.

[25] Teilhard de Chardin, *Pierre Teilhard de Chardin: Writings*, ed. and intro. Ursula King, Modern Spiritual Masters Series (Maryknoll, NY: Orbis Books, 2013), 115.

consciousness is a Christ capable of animating all traditions and for all time, a Christ that is *for* matter in the midst of matter, a Christ *for* and *of* humanity:

> After what will soon be two thousand years, Christ must be born again, he must be reincarnated in a world that has become too different from that in which he lived. Christ cannot reappear tangibly among us; but he can reveal to our minds a new and triumphant aspect of his former countenance.
>
> I believe that the Messiah whom we await, whom we all without any doubt await, is the universal Christ; that is to say, the Christ of evolution.[26]

Nothing less than unleashing this third dimension of Christ will suffice to support, within a Christian religious context, the efforts of the millennial generation toward building a society marked by a global inclusivity and equanimity. To ask this generation to exclude other faith traditions as invalid, or deny the inherent sacred value of *any* human being because of his or her sexual orientation or belief system, is simply incongruent with the very impetus that drives us. If Christianity is to survive, it must become a faith capable of enlivening all people and all religious traditions that seek the deepening and fostering of a global consciousness of love and unity or it will cease to animate humanity altogether.

Evolution and the Future

The millennial pragmatic idealism is self-evident in the rise of what researchers are describing as twenty-first-century capitalism; businesses run by or marketed to millennials are now categorized by a "second bottom line" in which businesses have a corresponding positive social or environmental impact tied into

---

[26] Teilhard de Chardin, *Christianity and Evolution*, 95.

their profit.[27] Millennials aren't willing to wait around passively for things to change but are actively and practically engaged in making the small incremental changes toward making their ideals a reality, and this is equally true within the context of religion. Humanity is ready to live into its own potential and to participate in mediating redemption. No longer a personal escape from the material world into an afterlife, the salvation humanity is now interested in is that of the betterment of the entire planet here and now.

Getting off the Bench

According to Teilhard, in human persons, evolution becomes conscious of itself,[28] establishing the direction of evolutionary convergence, a course that can only be observed over deep time. Teilhard believed that in humankind the goal of evolution can be glimpsed in the interiorization of evolution within the complexi-fied consciousness of humanity.[29] For the first time, in the human person, evolution becomes a *choice*.

> Evolution, by becoming conscious of itself in the depth of ourselves, only need to look at itself in the mirror to perceive itself in all its depths, and to decipher itself. In addition it becomes free to dispose of itself—it can give itself or refuse itself. Not only do we read in our slightest act the secret of its proceedings but for an elementary part we hold it in our hands, responsible for its past to its future.[30]

This perspective around the conditions necessary for further-ing evolution's potentiality, although contrary to the commonly held belief of evolution being biologically "blind," was later

---

[27] Burstein, *Fast Future*, 3.

[28] Teilhard de Chardin, *Activation of Energy*, 237.

[29] Pierre Teilhard de Chardin, *The Phenomenon of Man,* trans. Bernard Wall (New York: Harper and Row, 1959), 220–21.

[30] Ibid., 226.

correlated by scientists such as Jonas Salk. Salk postulated that evolution was deeply influenced not only by external conditions, but by specific interior environments that led to the formation of conscious thought, which he believed was the new frontier of evolution.[31] In a Christian perspective the conditions of Salk's "interior environment" and Teilhard's "evolution as choice" could be interpreted as Christ's redemptive invitation to participate in evolution by engendering Christ-consciousness within our selves and collectively, thereby giving our lives fully and creatively to the furthering of evolution's course. The redemptive act of Christ *is* the evolutive function of Christ, elevating the meaning of the cross to a new dimension, that of the cross of evolution itself:

> The Cross which is now the symbol not merely of the dark retrogressive side of the universe in genesis, but also and even more, of its triumphant and luminous side; the Cross which is the symbol of progress and victory won through mistakes, disappointments and hard work; the only Cross, in very truth, that we can honestly, proudly and passionately offer for the worship of a world that has become conscious of what it was yesterday and what awaits it tomorrow.[32]

In this redemption we are neither passive observers nor participants by an intellectual assent of a theological premise, but we participate by the very act of our will in the outpouring of our very lives. By deepening our collective consciousness we unleash the full capacity of our creativity and ingenuity, thereby becoming co-laborers with Christ.

> Everywhere he draws us to him and brings us closer to himself, in a universal movement of convergence toward

---

[31] Beatrix Murrel, "Consciousness in the Cosmos: Perspective of Mind: Jonas Salk," http://www.bixint.com/stoa_del_sol/conscious/conscious6.html.

[32] Teilhard de Chardin, *Christianity and Evolution*, 163.

spirit. It is he *alone* whom we seek and in whom we move. But if we are to hold him we must take *all things* to, and even beyond, the utmost limit of their nature and their capacity for progress. Of the cosmic Christ, we may say both that he is and that he is still growing.[33]

The Butterfly Effect

Teilhard provides an empowering hopeful message of the gospel congruent with the spirit of millennial pragmatic idealism: all of humanity forms the body of Christ, and creation eagerly awaits our awakening to our full potential (Romans 8:19). What we do with our lives matters *to* matter. Our choices affect not just our immediate environments but the whole global atmosphere in ways we are only beginning to comprehend in quantum physics. The experiments on quantum "entanglement" demonstrate that the quantum states of two or more objects operate in reference to one another even while separated spatially. In other words, everything truly *is* connected. If all of creation is quantumly entangled in this interabiding, the agency of our lives matters greatly indeed.

Just as the chaos theory's "butterfly effect," a metaphorical example in which flapping butterfly wings could result in the formation of a hurricane, our cosmos appears to be a system of relationships that are truly interdependent. The full potential and consequence of how our choices affect the evolution of consciousness has not fully dawned in the collective awareness. Thus far, humanity has understood the domino effect of our choices at a global scale by way of unprecedented participation in social and environmental causes, but we are still awaiting the full resonance of the spiritual heartbeat that can enliven and oxygenate what we intuitively care about, thereby revealing the source of all such good and just human ideals: the Christic heart of evolution.

---

[33] King, *Pierre Teilhard de Chardin*, 88.

Conclusion

What is occurring in our lifetimes is a major philosophical shift: from dogmatic institution into organic networking; from identifying as nationalistic to becoming globally and holistically minded; from a Newtonian static universe to the dynamism of a quantumly interconnected universe. If we want to remain faithful to Christianity's heart and message, we must begin the sacred labor of setting loose those aspects of the tradition that are simply incompatible with our cosmos; they continue to create an "intellectual and emotional straitjacket"[34] within which the creative force of an evolving humanity refuses to be restrained. It is imperative that, as socially responsible, intelligent followers of Christ we ask with Teilhard, "What form must our Christology take if it is to remain itself in a new world?"[35]

Within Teilhard's hyper-orthodoxy we can reimagine creation, incarnation, and redemption not simply as historical facts that can be localized in one point and time, but as quantumly cosmic dimensions that are *happening* and which we influence by our participation or refusal to participate.

> Christianity . . . is finally becoming alive to the fact that its three fundamental personalist mysteries are in reality simply the three aspects of one and the same process (Christogenesis) considered either in its motive principle (creation), or in its unifying mechanism (incarnation), or in its ascentional work (redemption); and so we find ourselves in the main stream of evolution.[36]

Teilhard's evolutionary theology allows for a Christology that deeply resonates with the Millennial generation and the spirit of modern humanity according to the following points:

- Creation is the risk of a God creating *through* evolution on a path from multiplicity to convergent unity, a risk we

---

[34] Teilhard de Chardin, *Christianity and Evolution*, 80.
[35] Ibid., 76.
[36] Ibid., 155.

ourselves undertake as we live, love, and create. Humanity is not the cause of a distortion of paradise, but the achievement of a universe in the act of becoming. Suffering and pain are no longer duality's foil that we seek to avoid at all costs, but the crux of our very humanity and the energetic process of our transformation.

- Incarnation is the union of matter and spirit, the embodiment of mystical divine potential that we each represent as individuals and as a collective "body." Christ no longer resides "out there," somehow separate from us. Neither is Christ located in one church building, denomination, or religious tradition over another. Christ is alive in the entire collective human family, in all of creation, as the catalyst of evolution.

- Redemption is the conscious choice of participation we make toward the furthering of evolution of consciousness through our will and through the offering of our human creativity toward that end. We are no longer passive recipients of the golden ticket to board the right theological train to heaven. We *are* the engine of heaven, of evolution itself, collaborating with Christ toward the fulfillment of the entire creation into Christ-Omega.

The time has come to release the constricting bonds of the first axial paradigm restraining Christianity's wings, not only to join the dynamism of our unfolding universe but to fill it in its expansion. We must employ all of our creativity, intellect, and spiritual efforts to revise dogma and write new liturgy, evolving that which is both contrary to the incarnational message and the millennial collective consciousness that is beginning to see *from and as* a whole. God and humanity can no longer be divided by an outdated construct of a static schism between spirit and matter, a trial of incompatible energies only rectified by the sacrificial lamb of Christ, perpetuating further dualities of "chosen" or "condemned." God must now emerge in our hearts as the very dynamism and interconnectivity of our universe by being understood inextricably *within* matter while infinitely *ahead* calling it toward its greatest convergent potential. Christ must be born again in our minds as the catalyst of all evolution, demonstrating the course of life through the energetic counterstrokes of pain and suffering, and resurrecting the whole of creation into a unified Christic body.

In Teilhard's hyper-orthodoxy all that was divided as sacred and secular forms but one singular unfolding story, a story that all generations can not only belong to but feel motivated to participate in; it is the story of God in the evolution of our cosmos, a story that is happening *now* and of which we are now part. The religious friction of our time has given birth to an electrically charged atmosphere of hope and possibility evident in the spirit of the millennial generation. Our time demonstrates the ripe conditions within which the spark of Teilhard's luminous theology could ignite the whole of humanity into a unified blazing heart. An evolutionary theology would not only address the pressing issues of our time by giving birth to a new comprehension of our collective consciousness, but would also mediate a new age of human creativity and ingenuity. What is emerging in our time is the desire for a faith *for* and *of* the earth, at long last capable of animating the fullness of our human potential, a potential fulfilled not in realizing divinity by rejecting our humanity, but rather of becoming more fully divine precisely *by becoming more fully human*. In the words of Teilhard,

> Let there be revealed to us the possibility of believing *at the same time and wholly* in God *and* the World, the one through the other; let this belief burst forth, as it is ineluctably in process of doing under the pressure of these seemingly opposed forces, and then, we may be sure of it, a great flame will illumine all things: for a Faith will have been born (or reborn) containing and embracing all others—and, inevitably, it is the strongest Faith which sooner or later must possess the Earth.[37]

---

[37] Pierre Teilhard de Chardin, *The Future of Man,* trans. Norman Deeny (New York: HarperCollins, 1964), 268.

8

The Eucharist as Liturgical Drama

Teilhard's "The Mass on the World"

KATHLEEN DUFFY, SSJ

Introduction

Philosopher Beatrice Bruteau was among the first American scholars to stimulate interest in Teilhard's thought. During the years immediately following the publication of the English translation of Teilhard's *Le phénomène humain*[1] and when his religious essays gradually became available, she steeped herself in his vision and began to develop some of the themes embedded in his growing opus. She was particularly interested in enhancing the symbolism that surrounds the great Christian mysteries and in showing their relevance to daily life.

Bruteau realized, as Teilhard did, that, more often than not, our spiritual insights pale in the light of the vastness and beauty of the cosmos. Even our ability to grasp the true space-time

---

[1] Pierre Teilhard de Chardin, *The Phenomenon of Man,* trans. Bernard Wall (New York: Harper and Row, 1959).

dimensions and creative power of the cosmos is inadequate. Thus, she suggests that meditation and ritual will stimulate our minds and hearts, awaken in us a sense of awe and wonder, and deepen our understanding of these great mysteries. Although finding ways to aptly celebrate them can be daunting, the importance of searching for models and experimenting with possibilities is paramount.

In the trenches of World War I and in the deserts of China, Teilhard found himself challenged to formulate such a ritual. Without the bread and wine needed for the eucharistic liturgy, he improvised and composed a dramatic liturgical poem, "The Mass on the World."[2] Although Bruteau does not often refer to Teilhard's "Mass" explicitly or consider its dramatic aspect, two of her major works, *The Easter Mysteries* and *The Holy Thursday Revolution*,[3] explore themes found in Teilhard's powerful poem. In this chapter I read Teilhard's "Mass" as a liturgical drama in which he weaves the mystery of the incarnation with his understanding of the evolutionary world, creating a synthesis that leads him to a profound act of surrender. I also show how Teilhard's "Mass" can be used as a liturgical ritual that speaks to our deepest spiritual and aesthetic yearnings.

The original version of Teilhard's "Mass," which he called "The Priest," was completed on July 8, 1918, while he was still serving as a stretcher bearer in World War I, and less than a month after he pronounced his solemn vows in the Jesuit house in Lyons.[4] His time in the trenches provided him life-challenging and life-changing experiences, but it also gave him time to sketch

---

[2] Pierre Teilhard de Chardin, *Writings in Time of War*, trans. René Hague (New York: Harper and Row, 1968), 119–34.

[3] Beatrice Bruteau, *The Easter Mysteries* (New York: Crossroad, 1995); Beatrice Bruteau, *The Holy Thursday Revolution* (Maryknoll, NY: Orbis Books, 2005).

[4] Teilhard de Chardin, *Writings in Time of War*, 203. In this essay I incorporate passages from both "The Priest" (Teilhard de Chardin, *Writings in Time of War*, 203–24) and "The Mass on the World" (Pierre Teilhard de Chardin, *The Heart of Matter*, trans. René Hague [New York: Harcourt Brace Jovanovich, 1978], 119–34).

out and to write down his vision in great detail. By that time the fruit of his struggle to find a God big enough to satisfy his insatiable thirst for the Universal[5] and to integrate the Christ of revelation with the theory of evolution had exploded into a cosmic vision that became almost too magnificent for him to hold.

In *The Divine Milieu*,[6] Teilhard shares his search for a God who not only fills the ever-expanding universe, but also embraces the entire cosmos:

> Is the Christ of the Gospels, imagined and loved within the dimensions of a Mediterranean world, capable of still embracing and still forming the centre of our prodigiously expanded universe? Is the world not in the process of becoming more vast, more close, more dazzling than Jehovah? Will it not burst our religion asunder? Eclipse our God?[7]

In other words, has our image of the universe become more ravishing than our image of God? Once Teilhard's mystical vision began to take shape, he felt a strong call to "spread abroad the Fire,"[8] to be an apostle of Christ in the universe. As we will see, Teilhard's "Mass" dramatizes his relationship with the "big enough God" he discovered, and celebrates his cosmic vision.

First performed in the trenches of the Forest of Laigue near Compiegne and Soissons, the "Mass" reached its final form in 1923 while Teilhard was searching for stone tools and fossils, in the Ordos Desert in Mongolia. This dramatic ritual, now even more fully developed, proved to be a creative way for Teilhard to celebrate the essence of the eucharistic liturgy in a cosmic key. Full of Christian imagery and tradition, the addition of a cosmic dimension lends Teilhard's "Mass" immense power. Throughout his life he continued to incorporate aspects of his "Mass" into his

---

[5] Teilhard de Chardin, *The Heart of Matter*, 22.

[6] Pierre Teilhard de Chardin, *The Divine Milieu: An Essay on the Interior Life*, trans. René Hague (New York: Harper and Row, 1968).

[7] Ibid., 46.

[8] Teilhard de Chardin, *Writings in Time of War*, 218.

daily liturgy. In fact, near the end of his life he wrote to his friend Jeanne Mortier that in a forthcoming essay, "The Christic," he hoped to integrate insights from his major mystical works: *The Divine Milieu*, his treatise on evolutionary spirituality, "The Heart of Matter," his autobiography, and "The Mass on the World," a dramatic interpretation of his cosmic vision.[9]

Teilhard's "Mass" opens with an overture, an invitation to worship that sets the stage for the three acts that follow: Act I: The Offertory, in which Teilhard finds himself embedded in the evolutionary cosmos searching for fitting gifts for the God of evolution; Act II: The Consecration, in which Teilhard sinks more deeply into the reality of the incarnation, eventually seeing evolution and incarnation as a single cosmic movement; and finally, Act III: The Communion, in which Teilhard commits himself to a continual transformation into Christ. The drama leaves him longing for the universal communion of all things in Christ.[10] In the dénouement, I consider the need for such rituals, and in the coda I suggest practical ways to celebrate Teilhard's "Mass" as dramatic ritual. We begin with the overture.

Overture: Invitation to Worship

Teilhard's "Mass" opens at dawn, a most precious moment of the day. Gradually and with no fanfare the morning light spills upward and the sky displays some of its most beautiful and softest hues. As our freshly painted earth awakens, she trembles, and with a prayer of hope-filled expectation for what might unfold during the coming day, she "once again begins her fearful travail."[11]

Overwhelmed by the beauty and sacredness of the morning and aware of his intimate connection to all of the characters in the almost fourteen-billion-year story of the universe, Teilhard summons the whole earth, of which he is a part, to join him in

---

[9] Teilhard de Chardin, *The Heart of Matter*, 80.
[10] Ibid., 94.
[11] Ibid., 120.

this liturgical ritual.[12] The sunrise, the landscape, and the vast mass of humanity appear on stage as vital actors in this ongoing drama: the rock and the sand that cradle the fossils of life, the fish that swim in a nearby stream, the warmth of the rising sun, the air that he breathes, even physical forces such as gravity and magnetism that cause both growth and decay, creative forces that foster union, violent forces that spread division, the inventive power of human thought, the warmth of human love, all servants to a process of universal becoming. Filled with a profound desire to be one with all creatures, Teilhard gathers them together in spirit: those that, like the fossils he is collecting, are "imprisoned in inert matter"; those who, like the newborn child, are just "opening their eyes to the light of life"; and those who, like his companions, "move and act in freedom."[13] Since "the only human embrace capable of worthily enfolding the divine is that of all men opening their arms to call down and welcome the Fire,"[14] he surrounds himself in spirit with humans from all corners of the globe—those dear to him and those he doesn't know, "the immense mass of undisciplined power" and the restless multitude that terrifies him.[15] Aware of himself as totally embedded within the cosmic becoming, Teilhard makes the whole earth his altar.[16]

Act I: Offertory:
Presenting the Fruits of the Creative Universe

Without the bread and wine needed for the eucharistic liturgy and aware of God's profound hunger and thirst for the good, the novel, and the beautiful, Teilhard searches for an appropriate gift. He chooses one that is most fitting—a universe that for almost

---

[12] Teilhard de Chardin, *Writings in Time of War,* 207.

[13] Ibid., 206.

[14] Teilhard de Chardin, *The Divine Milieu,* 144.

[15] Quoted in Thomas M. King, SJ, *Teilhard's Mass: Approaches to "The Mass on the World"* (New York: Paulist Press, 2005), 100, 101.

[16] Teilhard de Chardin, *The Heart of Matter,* 119.

fourteen billion years has been struggling to be transformed, a cosmos that, from the moment the blazing ball of energy flared forth, has been producing novel forms[17] through a process he calls creative union, matter's tendency to create by developing relationships. Simpler elements become more than they are by themselves as they unite with others and participate in a higher form of being. Though always creative, some processes of unification happen quickly and are violent, while others are more gentle and gradual. Examples abound: in the extreme heat of the core of the sun, nuclear fusion unites hydrogen nuclei to form a new element, helium; hydrogen and oxygen ions bond to form the water molecule with properties very different from its constituents; in the vast regions of space, clouds of gas and dust respond to the gravitational force to produce galaxies and stars. On earth the principle of creative union has also been guiding the evolution of life step by step from simple bacteria to a myriad of novel life forms. For instance, the zygote, formed from the union of sperm and egg, differs in shape and function from its component parts.

Teilhard places on his paten the abundant fruits of evolution, the harvest won by a daily renewal of labor.[18] In spirit, he gathers the marvelous successes of earth's many creatures, who little by little grope their way toward the light—bees who go from flower to flower gathering nectar to make honey, mothers who nurture their children in the womb, scientists who spend years searching for cures or designing labor-saving devices, all who strive each day to respond to the needs of a broken world. This bread will allay God's hunger.

Yet God also longs to be with those members of the cosmos who experience pain and suffering, the necessary consequence of an unfinished universe, and thirsts to comfort them. Therefore, Teilhard places in his chalice "the sap which is to be pressed out this day from the earth's fruits,"[19] the labor of birth, the false

---

[17] Ibid., 121.
[18] Ibid., 120.
[19] Ibid.

moves, the pain of the struggle, the anguish of death, all that evolution loses in exhaustion and suffering, as "caught between its passionate desire and its impotence," the cosmos groans and sets out to do the work of the coming day.[20] This wine will quench God's thirst.

Teilhard spreads his hands over the offerings, gifts from a universe filled with limitless joy and sorrow. In "the depth of a soul laid widely open to all the forces which . . . will rise . . . and converge upon the Spirit,"[21] he prays: "Take up in your hands, Lord, and bless this universe that is destined to sustain and fulfill the plenitude of your being among us."[22] Over all of creation, in whatever state it happens to be at the time, he calls down the Fire.[23]

Act II: The Consecration: The Spiritual Power of Matter

The Fire! The raging Fire that from the very beginning of time has been blazing at the heart of matter! The radiant Word, illuminating the darkness; the divine Spirit, breathing "a soul into the newly formed, fragile film of matter";[24] the divine Presence, energizing the cosmos from within! In the beginning there was Fire—"intelligent, loving, energizing"[25] Power—the Fire of the incarnation that penetrated the original fireball that flared forth and that, blazing at the heart of matter, has been *"immortalizing and unifying the cosmos ever since."*[26] Teilhard prepares to celebrate this mystery.

Mindful of the hopes and dreams of the entire cosmic community, with all of its longing to become, he spreads his hands

---

[20] Teilhard de Chardin, *Writings in Time of War*, 206.
[21] Teilhard de Chardin, *The Heart of Matter*, 120.
[22] Teilhard de Chardin, *Writings in Time of War*, 207.
[23] Teilhard de Chardin, *The Heart of Matter*, 121.
[24] Ibid., 122.
[25] Ibid., 121–22.
[26] Ibid., 90.

over every living thing that will spring up, grow, flower, or ripen during the day, and with deep reverence and awe, he pronounces those utterly transformative words: "This is my Body." Then, strengthened by the Bread of Life, the love of his friends, and the authenticity of his call, Teilhard lifts the chalice and, "over every death-force which waits in readiness to corrode, to wither, to cut down," he says: "This is my Blood."[27] Once again, the Divine radiates from within the terrifying totality of things as the world is made flesh and becomes a living flame!

Then, in "an explosion of dazzling flashes,"[28] Teilhard realizes that the evolutionary convergence of the cosmos and the gradual emergence of the Cosmic Christ within the evolutionary process are but two faces of a single movement.[29] The whole universe is being amorized, personalized,[30] transformed into the Body of Christ, and Christ is becoming the Soul of the World.[31]

Because of the incarnation, Teilhard knows that if he truly believes that everything around him is the Body and Blood of the Word, he will be able to recognize the luminous warmth of Christ that shines forth "from the depths of every element, every encounter, every event,"[32] allowing him to plunge into Christ, to touch Christ, to be cradled in Christ's loving arms.[33] Because he desires the incarnate Christ with his whole being, he finds that he can no longer breathe outside this milieu.

Teilhard asks for faith.

Act III: Communion: Transformation

Teilhard is moved to adore. But once the Fire pierces his heart, he realizes that he must do more than contemplate the great eu-

---

[27] Ibid., 123.
[28] Ibid., 50.
[29] Ibid., 82.
[30] Ibid., 83.
[31] Ibid., 124.
[32] Ibid., 127.
[33] Ibid., 125–26.

charistic mystery. He must also "consent to the communion,"[34] to "communion with God through earth"[35] with all the terror that this acceptance entails.[36] To commit to the future is a terrifying thing; the task is too large; the way is unknown. Our world is unfinished, still in a process of becoming, sometimes behaving like a "seething cauldron," a whirlpool of conflicts and energies, an aggregate of disparate and antagonistic elements all "brewed together." Seemingly incurable divisions and innate hostilities make the dream of a united world look impossible.[37] Yet despite its outward appearance of fragmentation and division, the cosmos is becoming the Body of Christ.[38] Beneath a surface of incoherence and hopeless plurality, a "living and deep-rooted unity" is trying to break free.[39] To facilitate the release of this energy entails struggle. Teilhard knew intimately the struggle inherent in any work of creation—digging for fossils and stone tools requires strenuous physical labor; interpreting and integrating the masses of available data requires patience and perseverance; articulating an innovative mystical vision requires strenuous mental rigor; engaging in dialogue with superiors who fail to see one's point requires extreme spiritual stamina.

Aware of the cost, aware of the gain, Teilhard considers the choice before him. To take the Bread, to drink the Wine is to surrender his ego, to face danger, to open himself to new ideas, to purify his affections.[40] To eat is to relish the gifts of creation and to acquire a taste for the mystical; to drink is to accept the forces of dissolution and to submit to processes of diminishment

---

[34] Ibid., 127.

[35] Teilhard de Chardin, *Writings in Time of War*, 57–71.

[36] This moment of terror is one that Kant would define as sublime. See Thomas Weiskel, *The Romantic Sublime: Studies in the Structure and Psychology of Transcendence* (Baltimore: The Johns Hopkins University Press, 1976).

[37] Teilhard de Chardin, *Writings in Time of War*, 205.

[38] Ibid., 208.

[39] Ibid., 205.

[40] Teilhard de Chardin, *The Heart of Matter*, 130. This liturgical drama finally arrives at a moment of anagnorisis, a moment of realization.

and death.[41] Suddenly, he is beset with existential dread. He prays that his terror might be turned into joy at the thought of being transformed into Christ. He hears Christ call: Eat! Drink! How can he refuse?

We arrive at the climax. Longing to be united with Christ at the heart of matter, Teilhard resolves to accept the challenge. He stretches out his hands and reaches for the fiery Bread, the seed of the future. He takes it; eats it. He lays his whole being wide open to Christ's inspiration. The Bread reaches out to him and draws him to Itself;[42] he is grasped by Christ. Rather than escaping from the world like the mystics of old, he resolves to plunge into earth, to mingle with created things, to seize hold of them. He commits himself to listen attentively to the aspirations and the groans of the entire earth community and to work assiduously to further greater consciousness of the evolutionary goal of unity.

Again, he hears the word: Drink! Suddenly all of the forces that have battered him, all of the pain that they have inflicted on him become a touch of God's hands.[43] He reaches for the Wine. He takes it; he drinks. He delivers himself in utter abandon to those fearful forces that frighten him, entrusts himself to the great ocean of energies he can never control. Assured of Christ's constant care and inspiration, he yields "in blissful surrender,"[44] vows to heed Christ's least promptings by taking seriously whatever stimulates him, whatever attracts him, whatever wounds him, until he can truly say: "Whatever happens is adorable."[45] He knows now that earth will clasp him in her loving arms, and that, in the end, resting in the bosom of the One who loves him, he will "contemplate the face of God."[46]

Prostrate before the divine Presence and filled with impassioned love for Christ hidden in the forces of earth, he surrenders

---

[41] Ibid.

[42] Teilhard de Chardin, *Writings in Time of War*, 215.

[43] Teilhard de Chardin, *The Heart of Matter*, 122.

[44] Teilhard de Chardin, *Writings in Time of War*, 215.

[45] Quoted in King, *Teilhard's Mass*, 107.

[46] Teilhard de Chardin, *The Heart of Matter*, 130, 129.

himself to the one who holds all things together and cries out: "Lord, make us *one*."[47]

Dénouement

Teilhard's love for the eucharistic mystery is deep; his synthesis, profound. In his "Mass," evolution and incarnation become a single cosmic drama, a single movement toward the future. This weaving of the story of the evolutionary becoming with the mystery of the incarnation allows for greater access to the divine Light that is shining through all of creation.[48] Yet, since Teilhard's cosmic insights are still not universally understood, the need to make Teilhard's approach to the "Mass" accessible is vital.

Coda

Both Teilhard and Bruteau encourage the use of ritual as a way of allowing the process of cosmic becoming to seep into our consciousness and thus to ready us to participate more fully in the sacred drama that is our daily life. But the questions remain: How can we convert Teilhard's dramatic essay into a ritual that will open our minds and hearts to the wonders of the cosmos and the greatness of the Cosmic Christ? How do we perform the ritual in a way that will draw us into the mystery and then also plunge us into the drama of life? How do we celebrate Teilhard's insights without devising a rote ritual that grows tired with age, without using ideas that sound abstract and words that are unfamiliar? We now explore some examples that have been tried and suggest other possibilities.

In *Teilhard's Mass* the late Jesuit Thomas King suggests a way of incorporating key passages from Teilhard's essay into

---

[47] Ibid., 121.

[48] Beatrice Bruteau, *Evolution toward Divinity: Teilhard de Chardin and the Hindu Traditions* (Wheaton, IL: The Theosophical Publishing House, 1974), 27.

the eucharistic liturgy,[49] as he often did during his lifetime. These passages accentuate the major elements of the "Mass" and add a cosmic flavor to the eucharistic celebration. To make the experience more accessible, King simplifies the text, provides an alternate introduction for those who prefer to celebrate in the evening, and is quite strategic about where he places the passages within the "Mass" so as not to violate its integrity.[50] He also suggests ways of using the text as part of a prayer service instead.

On the other hand, a dramatic reading of the text can be quite effective. An early example is John Crane's 1974 dramatic reading of the entire text of Teilhard's "Mass" interspersed very effectively with violin music.[51] On April 9, 2015, at Georgetown University, in celebration of sixtieth anniversary of Teilhard's death, Frank Frost and others prepared and performed a dramatic reading of major selections from Teilhard's "Mass." Music and photography enhanced the ritual and helped to communicate to the audience the deeper meaning behind some of Teilhard's most profound passages;[52] there is also an excerpt from a dramatic reading of Teilhard's "Mass" in Chinese.[53] Set in the Ordos Desert, a site where the "Mass" was celebrated, the performance transports the listener to the original scene and enhances the sacred nature of the words. Other rituals, such as the one performed as the end of the 2005 conference, "Rediscovering Teilhard's Fire," at Chestnut Hill College, combine elements of music, dance, art work, and photography, media that are often capable of communicating at a deeper level than words.

Besides including excerpts from the "Mass" into an actual eucharistic liturgy or staging a dramatic reading of excerpts from

---

[49] King, *Teilhard's Mass*, 159–66.

[50] Ibid., 159.

[51] Pierre Teilhard de Chardin, "Hymn of the Universe (1): Mass on the World," audiobook (1974). To locate a library near you with a copy of the recording, check www.worldcat.org.

[52] Excerpts from the dramatic reading of "The Mass on the World," YouTube video, performed at Georgetown University, April 9, 2015.

[53] A YouTube video of an excerpt is available; the full "Mass" is part of a "Teilhard and China" DVD, available from the Ricci Institute.

the text, preparing stirring rituals to celebrate with family and friends on special days or to grieve with them at times of great sorrow connects the most ordinary and most intimate moments of our lives to the evolutionary becoming of the cosmos and to the God who is leading us into the future. In any case, focusing on the cosmic community as a whole even while celebrating or mourning with a segment of the cosmic community and situating the ritual within a setting surrounded by music, art, dance, and other media will enhance the celebration.

Perhaps the simplest way to use Teilhard's "Mass" is as a private daily ritual, either as part of the eucharistic liturgy itself or as a morning prayer. Recalling the major elements of his "Mass" can lead one gently but deeply into the mystery of the incarnation: setting an all-inclusive scene, gathering the earth community, calling to mind our own joys and sorrows as well as those of the rest of the cosmic community, offering these to Christ knowing that Christ will transform them, taking the Bread, grateful for Christ's presence in all things and thankful for the nourishment of the day, taking the Wine, receiving the pain transformed and being willing to accept whatever awaits us in the day ahead.

Of course, the ritual is not an end in itself. True ecstasy comes from participating in the divine Life, by caring for earth's many creatures, by working for unity, and most especially by co-creating with the Cosmic Christ.

PART III

TEACHER, MENTOR, FRIEND

*Love alone is capable of uniting living beings
in such a way as to complete and fulfill them,
for it alone takes them and joins them by
what is deepest in themselves.*
—Pierre Teilhard de Chardin

9

A Grateful Reader

John Shea

In the 1970s and 1980s I was directing a doctor of ministry program and teaching systematic theology. Consequently, I was always on the lookout for well-written material to give to students. I came across a number of articles in *Cistercian Studies, Cross Currents,* and *The Journal of Christian Healing* that connected scripture, especially the Gospels, with the theories and practices of spiritual development from Western and Eastern sources and were suffused with the sense of a new cultural moment in cosmic and social evolution. They were written in an accessible and engaging way and proved to be great triggers for creative and critical pastoral conversations. The author was Beatrice Bruteau.

I managed to find a telephone number for Beatrice. On the phone I told her how much I enjoyed her articles and how I was using them. I also asked if she could send me a bibliography of her work. She asked, "Are you a serious reader?"

I remember being taken back by that question. I do not remember exactly what I replied, but whatever it was, it was enough. The bibliography arrived in the mail along with a number of issues of *The Roll,* the newsletter of *Schola Contemplationis.* I started to read.

Over the next couple of years I got to know Beatrice and her husband, Jim Somerville. I finagled an invitation, and she came to lecture at Mundelein Seminary. I introduced her to Mike Leach, a long-time friend, who at the time was president of the Crossroad/ Continuum Publishing Group in New York City, and their productive relationship began. I played a supportive role in assuring the editorial staff at the University of Notre Dame Press that the essays in *The Grand Option* were important contributions. When I was in North Carolina, I met with Beatrice and Jim; when they were in Chicago, they had dinner at my apartment with Anne, me, and a few others. At Beatrice's invitation I published a long poem on John the Baptist in one of the issues of *The Roll*. I substituted for her at a conference in San Francisco—making an inappropriate remark about the very small (Beatrice) and the very large (me). Occasionally, we talked on the phone—never short conversations. However, as my life moved in a different direction, we did not keep up our personal contact.

Her Writing

But I kept in touch with her through her writings, always remembering the burden and promise of the serious reader. In the process I increasingly became what I was from the beginning—a grateful reader. There always seemed to be a connection between what Beatrice was writing and where my mind was beginning to go, and she often provided the next mental step that I was not capable of making on my own. She stretched me in the right directions.

Also, I just liked the way she wrote. She herself was never far from her text. She would often engage in self-disclosure, a frank evaluation of how she arrived at a particular point of view. For pages on end I often had the impression I was sitting across from her and she was pouring her passion and conviction into me, admitting in one breath that what she was saying was not universally acknowledged and, in the next breath, admitting that in her opinion it should be and would eventually be. She had a confidence in her own experience and rationality, and she conveyed that confidence to readers. In the area of spirituality a teacher whose confidence comes from both her own experience and reflection, as well as her inheritance of traditions, is powerful.

But this confidence was not an egocentric sense of being right. Rather, it was the exhilaration of following the clues that experience, science, and multiple spiritual traditions had left scattered on the ground. I think what kept me attentive as I read sentence after sentence was this underlying sense of detective work. She was "onto something," and her readers were Watsons to her Holmes. The game was definitely afoot, and we were together in the chase. Quite simply, she wrote on a roll.

Thank You

So, this essay does not attempt to position Beatrice in the emerging literature of interspirituality, or to show the combination of indebtedness to other thinkers and her own originality, or to make a case for her contribution to the future connections of spirituality, cosmos, and social change—as important as those efforts are. It is simply a thank you from one individual who knew her personally and read her seriously.

There is so much to be thankful for in her wide-ranging writings—creatively interpreting the Christian doctrines of Incarnation, Trinity, Theotokos, and Child of God, providing philosophic coherence to sociological and scientific findings, exploring how psychic grids are built up and dismantled, bringing together diverse dialogue partners like Teilhard de Chardin and the Hindu traditions, spelling out in detail what discipleship to Jesus entails, conducting interfaith conversations, rewording the dense language of mystical consciousness to make it accessible to lesser mortals, and so on. There is a great deal to acknowledge, and all of it resources those of us who are interested in spirituality, faith traditions, and contemporary culture.

But in this essay I want to scale down my appreciation to three areas—scriptural insights, maps of psycho-spiritual states, and the metaphysical/social connection. These areas not only helped me personally, but I was able to use them in my work. I am a theological educator, and the way Beatrice developed these areas provided solid background theory and also helped me create inputs and exercises that made the educational process more incisive and effective. Finally, I want to share the bigger picture in which I see Beatrice and her work.

Scriptural Insights

For years I worked with Christian teachers and preachers on how to use scripture in their ministries.[1] This entailed reading scripture scholars and selecting from their erudition images, ideas, and strategies that could be imported into the pastoral activity of teaching and preaching. As one preacher put it, "The pickings are slim." But in Beatrice's writings the pickings were abundant. The scriptural interpretations that are spread throughout her work are a rich resource for preachers and teachers.

At times Beatrice gives instructions on how to meditate on gospel passages based on her own meditation experiences. But, for the most part, she does not approach scriptural texts as spiritual practices or the objects of careful line-by-line scrutiny. Rather, they are inserted into larger philosophical, theological, and mystical contexts. I have found these "houses" for specific passages illuminating and provocative.

For example, in *The Holy Thursday Revolution*, Beatrice develops the idea that people who hold the view that suffering is the result of sin are hampered in their ability to hear Jesus's call to make things better. When the well-off are blessed by God because of their virtue and the suffering are punished by God because of their sin, the logical response is to stand back and judge. This hardened structure of thought has prohibited people from action-oriented responses to the proclamation of the kingdom.

---

[1] This work produced four volumes, *The Spiritual Wisdom of the Gospels for Christian Preachers and Teachers* (Collegeville, MN: Liturgical Press, 2004, 2005, 2006, 2010).

With this rendition of the latent functioning of a sin-suffering model, she offered a specific story from the Gospel of Mark.

> In the story of the paralyzed man who was let down through the roof, we find the link between sin and suffering and the action of Jesus can be interpreted as a definitive dissolution of that link. The assumption of the people observing this event was that the man must be a great sinner to be so handicapped, so Jesus' first response to the situation is to declare the man free from sin. Released from the belief that he is under God's curse, the man is no longer paralyzed but is able to do useful work. The message to the nation is: Stop believing that our present condition is our fate. God is not against us but for us. Don't think we are paralyzed. We can do something to help ourselves. We can![2]

This rousing call to action is not the standard way this text is interpreted. Most interpretations assume Jesus is working within the sin-suffering model and, with his God powers, forgiving the sin and thereby relieving the suffering. Beatrice suggests that he is destroying the model and is more radical and thus more appealing to contemporary sensibilities.

Another example is the mystical context she develops to interpret the simple description that the beloved disciple is reclining on the breast of Jesus (John 13:23). The beloved disciple is not looking at Jesus. He is coinciding with him and looking out with him. Beatrice glosses what this means, and it is worth citing at length for it is the key to discipleship.

> In order to move closer to the heart of Jesus, we "lean back toward him" by sinking back into the depth of our own consciousness, sinking down toward the center of our being. . . . Each deeper level that we sink to, position our sense of "I" in, brings us closer to the heart or center of

---

[2] Beatrice Bruteau, *The Holy Thursday Revolution* (Maryknoll, NY: Orbis Books, 2005), 208.

Jesus, because it is bringing us closer to our own center.
. . . The consciousness of Jesus, the interior of his heart,
is becoming more and more "available" to us, "known"
to us, "familiar to us—because our own heart is sharing
those same dispositions. We are coming to know the Sacred
Heart from the inside, inside his consciousness, and inside
our consciousness. . . . We cannot know it as *another*, as
something that stands opposite to us that we look at. That
is why we do not face Jesus in order to move closer to him,
but rather back into him. Were we to face him we would
always remain outside him. "Looking at" would turn him
into an object. . . . To know the subject, you have to enter
inside the subject, enter into the subject's own awareness,
that is, have that awareness in your own subjectivity: "Let
that mind be in you which was also in Christ Jesus." (Phi-
lippians 2:5)[3]

The implications of this insight into the Johannine image of the
beloved disciple reclining on the breast of Jesus re-envisions the
path of discipleship and any understanding of Christian spirituality based on following Jesus.

These are just two examples of the scriptural insights that
are rife in the writings of Beatrice Bruteau. To read Beatrice is
continually to encounter fresh approaches to familiar scriptural
texts, approaches that make sense of the texts and at the same
time bring us into a theological and often mystical vision of
reality. Christian preachers and teachers think people are ready
and waiting for this type of scripturally based spiritual wisdom.

Psycho-Spiritual Maps

Anyone who teaches theology in educational settings, pastoral
settings, or organizational settings has to deal with moral impera-
tives. In Christian literature litanies of virtues and vices are com-

---

[3] Beatrice Bruteau, *Radical Optimism: Rooting Ourselves in Reality*
(New York: Crossroad, 1993), 98–99.

monplace, often accompanied by strong statements of positive and negative consequences. But the psycho-spiritual component of these virtues and vices is not very well developed. We do not know the internal dynamics of compassion and self-centeredness, of violence and peacefulness, of retaliation and forgiveness, and so on. Without insights into these internal struggles we are reduced to mechanically repeating the importance of virtue and excoriating the individual and social effects of vices. As Beatrice puts it in a number of places, you cannot ask for new behavior from an old identity. You have to reconstruct the identity to allow the new behavior to emerge. In order to support our freedom and our choices, we need better renditions of all that is involved in the complex game of thought, feeling, and action.

Beatrice's writings provide just that. They take their time to describe psycho-spiritual states that influence moral behavior. These descriptions detail how interior ideas, attitudes, and feelings come together to produce permeating perspectives and dispositions. They also play out sequences, mini dramas of how these psychological states rise and fall. These maps are so well drawn that they become mirrors for readers who can see themselves within the dramas. I seldom get through a whole description without pausing, putting the book down, and checking out my own experience using the magnifying glass of the text. Reading Beatrice is always a journey of self-discovery, sometimes wanted and sometimes not.

A sample of the psychological states she unpacks includes how we identify and disidentify with our descriptive selves, how an interior journey will bring us to coincide with the spiritual identity of "I am that may you be," how a narrow consciousness leads to isolation and competition, how I-I relationships are possible, how creative freedom and choice freedom are distinguished and connected, how the logic of mutual negation reinforces our sense of separateness, how the cultural default of domination is internalized, how community is the essential condition of the reality of persons, how an emphasis on the future self is crucial to the courage to forgive, and more. Although these areas of experience and others she chooses are not the "usual suspects" for introspection, they are critically important for in-depth identity and mission. Beatrice is a gifted practitioner of phenomenological description, painting numerous pictures of how our consciousness works and how it could work in different ways, ways that would be more faithful to the metaphysical truths about ourselves and to how we are called to contribute to social and cosmic reality.

A particular psycho-spiritual map is usually not described in only one place. It often appears again and again, in different books and in different contexts. For example, a map of how we identify and disidentify with our descriptive selves is sketched in a 1977 article and in at least five books, the last, according to my fallible reckoning, published in 2005. But this is not repetition. She is reflecting on the psycho-spiritual experience, going over the same territory but enhancing the description by deepening and expanding it.

One of the psycho-spiritual states she develops in a number of places is how *eros* and *agape* interrelate within our experience. When she focused on this psycho-spiritual map, she often just noted the contrast between *eros* as loving for the sake of the lover and *agape* as loving for the sake of the beloved. But in *God's Ecstasy* she charts their dynamic unfolding:

> The bond of the community is love, especially agape love. But look at the dynamic of personal being even from the point of view of erotic love. Eros desires to be united with the other (as a good for oneself). Many erotic relationships begin with desire for the descriptions of the other, but if the desire runs deep, if there is strong attraction to the other as person, then an interesting thing happens. One is not satisfied with merely being intimate with the descriptive reality of the other. One wants to be close to the interior of the other, to feel the other on the inside, as the other feels. One yearns to be with the other not as the other appears to be but as the other really is from the other's own profound sense of self. How can we achieve that? We have to abandon our own point of view and strive to enter into the beloved's point of view, to see and feel as the beloved's

own welfare together with the beloved. But that is agape. If you really want to fulfill yourself, you have to abandon yourself and enter another. Isn't that amazing?[4]

As I read it, the logic of the unfolding is this: if persons begin with eros—loving another for the benefits they receive—and follow carefully where that love leads them, they will find themselves pulled into agape—loving another for the good of the one loved. The final paradoxical flourish is that loving the other for the other's good is how lovers find their own fulfillment. Losing their life, they find it.

However, Beatrice cannot resist stepping out of this description and commenting, "Isn't that amazing?" Besides the very sage tracking of how love consciousness unfolds, the sheer wonder of the love dynamics catches her and she wants readers to participate in her amazement. So she invites them in. It worked for me. When I used this eros-agape map to see my love relationships, there was enough of a fit for me to be amazed by this subtle beckoning to something more that accompanies what I thought was my preferential quest. Could it be that we are seduced into the ultimate reality we are even when we follow a path prescribed by a lesser rendition of ourselves? That, I surmise, is providential pressure, the patient and persistent lure that brings us into the consciousness that the loss of the erotic self is the finding of the agapic self. We become who we most are—what Beatrice calls "the secret self," "the naked self," "the bottommost self"—by paying attention to the lures built into the dynamics of our love experiences.

The Metaphysical/Social Connection

For the last ten years I have been engaged in leadership formation with senior executives in Catholic Health Care and affiliated organizations. A significant aspect of this formation is the

---

[4] Beatrice Bruteau, *God's Ecstasy: The Creation of a Self-Creating World* (New York: Crossroad, 1997), 30.

connection between metaphysical truths and social expressions. The twin foundations of the Catholic social tradition are human dignity and common good. These philosophically articulated convictions are derived from the theological truths of revelation—what Beatrice named the child of God (human dignity) and the trinitarian nature of personhood (common good). The responsibility of the leader is to hold these truths and allow them to affirm and challenge individual behaviors and social policies. The metaphysical truths are driven to find creative individual and social manifestations.

Beatrice spelled out this connection in eloquent ways. In *The Holy Thursday Revolution* she interpreted the ministry of Jesus from this perspective.[5] The metaphysical truth that animated Jesus was that each person was a child of God. This conviction galvanized Jesus into a social program of boundary breaking. The society in which Jesus lived was not set up on a foundation of universal divine filiation. It was divided in ways that ignored and even rejected this common basis. So Jesus broke these boundaries as part of the manifestation of the deeper metaphysical truth. He broke the boundaries between religious/ethnic groups, rich and poor, authorities and common people, diseased and healthy, men and women, even between friends and enemies. As Saint Paul would put it, "There is no longer Jew or Greek, there is no longer slave or free, there is no longer male or female; for all of you are one in Christ Jesus" (Gal 3:28). Allowing theological conviction to prosecute social arrangements is central to the mission of traditions that seek to continue the revelation of the life, death, and resurrection of Jesus.

But Beatrice went deeper. She put this metaphysical/social connection into the essential structure of human persons. When we have learned to disidentify with our biological and social descriptions and arrive at the sheer "I am" of our spiritual identity, we discover we are meant to incarnate ourselves in the processes of the world. The "I am" unfolds into "may you be."

---

[5] Bruteau, *The Holy Thursday Revolution*, 53–58.

Our incarnate life in the world is a process: it flows, it improvises like a skillful musician, it creates a work of art. When our consciousness enters completely into the realization of ourselves as free to love all equally and to unite with the whole, we experience the artistic development of the human process and world process as fulfilling the divine creative act. This will include all types and levels of our human activity, our economic and ecological arrangements, our social relations, our scientific and technical explorations and inventions, our artistic expressions.[6] Spiritual identity and all types of incarnation, including ethical behavior and social policy, are two sides of the same coin. If you are concerned with social change for greater dignity and common good, its secret energy is your spiritual identity. And if you embody your spiritual identity, you will participate in the transformation of self and society. If I may be so bold, you have Beatrice's word on it.

The Secret Purposes of God

In *A Secular Age* Charles Taylor talks about the diversity of spiritual development within a religious tradition.

It goes without saying that for most people who undergo a conversion there may never have been one of those seemingly self authenticating experiences . . . but they may easily take on a new view about religion from others: saints, prophets, charismatic leaders, who have radiated some sense of more direct contact.

The sense that others have been closer is an essential part of the ordinary person's confidence in a shared religious language, or a way of articulating fullness. These may be named figures, identified paradigms, like Francis

---

[6] Beatrice Bruteau, "Global Spirituality and Integration of East and West," in *The Grand Option: Personal Transformation and a New Creation* (Notre Dame, IN: University of Notre Dame Press, 2001), 124.

of Assisi, or Saint Teresa; or Jonathan Edwards, or John Wesley; or they may figure as the unnamed company of (to oneself) unknown saints or holy people. In either case (and often these two are combined), the language one adheres to is given force by the conviction that others have lived in a more complete, direct and powerful manner. This is part of what it means to belong to a church.[7]

For me, Beatrice is one of those people who gives force and conviction to our shared religious language because she has plumbed its depths and found a complementary language to articulate its life-giving wisdom. She has creatively reinterpreted the wellsprings of the Christian revelation by dialoging with other mystical traditions and science. When I assimilate what she has said, even though I cannot comprehend all of it, I can feel the energies of life and love to which she testifies. I like being part of a tradition that has her in it. But there is a further wild thought that I cannot quite stop from entertaining.

In *Cat's Cradle* Kurt Vonnegut whimsically suggests that God has organized the world into Karasses, groups of people who serve one of God's purposes. A Karass may consist of a few people or many. They may know the purpose they serve or the purpose may be only suspected. They may be very advanced in their service or bumbling amateurs. However, there is one thing about members of a Karass: if and when they meet they will feel a kinship, even though they may not be able to completely explain it. They will begin to talk, sensing their conversation will serve the divine purpose but not knowing exactly how.

As I read Beatrice and watch her draw from the works of other people as if they were all weaving the same tapestry with different colored thread, I suspect something like a Karass is at work. And when Beatrice's work becomes more widely known, other people—from all faith traditions and no faith traditions

---

[7] Charles Taylor, *A Secular Age* (Cambridge, MA: The Belknap Press of Harvard University, 2007), 729.

at all—will feel a kinship. They will be drawn to what she says. This intuitive kinship will be enough to keep them reading. In this way the Karass will grow in influence and the divine purpose will be served. And they may become what I am now—a grateful reader.

10

The Ecstasy of the Dancer and Perichoresis

A Tribute to Beatrice Bruteau

Carla DeSola

As a new and budding Catholic I came upon Beatrice Bruteau almost by happenstance, not realizing what a deep impact she would have theologically on me, a sacred dancer. She became a true spiritual mentor and friend; we never really had overt theological conversations, but it was the fabric of our relationship. We kept in touch over the years through her invitations to attend programs at Fordham University, conferences for which she invited me to dance, and socially through dinners with my mother. I also visited her when she moved to North Carolina in her later years. During one visit she even helped me organize an essay on liturgical dance that I was asked to compose.

I am writing this essay as an offering of love and appreciation for Beatrice, who was a real inspiration to me. I realize there is a huge gap between what she has given to the world through the power of her thought and writings and my attempt, in a small way, to give flesh to who she was as a person, one who happened to befriend a young dancer seeking God. In this essay, however,

I touch upon her role in my life, including the challenge of her as a theologian in conversation with me as a sacred dancer; as well as some thoughts on giving flesh to perichoresis as a dancer.

Our relationship began when James Somerville, then a Jesuit priest at Fordham University (and later her husband), invited Beatrice to be present at my baptism. As our relationship grew, she encouraged me to honor both my Jewish heritage and my budding Catholicism. Beatrice loved to dance, and she would play Jewish folk music so we could dance together. She was also proud to show off various Yoga poses that she practiced with a neighborhood boy.

Whenever I had theological or spiritual questions, I would call Beatrice; she would present illuminating thoughts that, at the time, I did not realize were unusual or radical but in later years would be awestruck by her depth and perspective on spiritual matters. She would urge me to pray in various ways, I think influenced by her background in Vedanta as well as Catholic spirituality. Many turns and directions in my life were a result of her invitations to contribute dance to various religious events as well as her visionary ideas.

Beatrice's insights began to shape how I thought about dance. One time I was questioning her about communion, and because she knew how much movement spoke to me, she asked me to imagine a presider who, while holding up the host, would not only look directly at it, but also move the host in such a way—slowly from side to side—so that the whole congregation would feel included as the one body of Christ. Another teaching, which she offered years later, in her eighties, emerged while eating at her favorite cafeteria. She would take a few bites from her plate, jump up and visit tables all around her, getting to know the people, particularly hugging the children. I was usually embarrassed by Beatrice's behavior, but a woman at her memorial service remarked that this was her way of sharing communion. When someone asked me recently what Beatrice was like, I immediately recalled this action. Her interior happiness was shown outwardly, generously shared with others.

This was reminiscent in her writings when she described God's relation to creation.

Many of my comments have been inspired by Beatrice's book *God's Ecstasy,* particularly the section "The Theocosmic Exegete."[1] You might wonder why a dancer, choreographer, and teacher of sacred dance is reading such material? And why do I quote the following paragraph to almost every class I teach at the Graduate Theological Union in Berkeley? Here is a kernel of Beatrice's thought, which I shall develop from the vantage point of a sacred dancer:

> This is what I am calling "ecstasy," the insideness turning into outsideness. It can also be called exegesis, manifestation, revelation, showing, phenomenalization. It has been likened to speech, to "uttering" what has been "hidden." I myself like best to liken it to dancing, because the dance is precisely the dancer, in the act of dancing. The dance movements and gestures are outsideness for the dancer; they are phenomenon, things shown. But they are revelatory of the dancer. They are contingent upon the dancer and the dancer transcends them all, but the dancer is really present in and as them. The dancer's inside turns into the outsideness of the dance when the dancer dances. This turning inside out is ecstasy. I am suggesting that this is God's relation to the cosmos. The cosmos is a kind of dancing revelation of God. It is a kind of offspring of God. It is a kind of speech of God. It is a kind of phenomenalization of God. It is a kind of incarnation of God. God creates the world as an act of agape-ecstasy.[2]

The quotation is revelatory. How do I dance so that my "insideness" becomes "outsideness"? Beatrice surmises that the

---

[1] Beatrice Bruteau, *God's Ecstasy: The Creation of a Self-Creating World* (New York: Crossroad, 1997), 39.

[2] Ibid.

dance movements express the insideness of the dancer. My first thought, however, was that while the insideness becomes the outsideness in the dance, as Beatrice notes, what is revealed in the dance is still not necessarily *who* the person is, nor does the dance have the capacity to be an act of revelation for others. The sacred dancer needs to know where her movements come from. For the dancer, being one with your true depth of being is a process. Dance reveals who you are at any particular stage of your spiritual journey. The "lover unites with beloved" just as she is, with stumbling and bravado, falls and peaks of movement—God being equally in the soaring, suspended leap and curled in the shell of a spent performer. Dance is a metaphor for God's ecstatic love, but the dancer must develop her insideness by being deeply in touch with her own interior self. Only in this way does she reveal the insideness of God. In other words, dance does reveal who one is, but it does not necessarily reveal the depth of who one is.

Dance Meditation

The desire to dance or choreograph from a depth of consciousness and freedom has led me to develop a course in dance meditation. The mind alone cannot embody this consciousness. When I teach dance meditation, I pray with my class:

> Dear God, in whom we live and move and have our being. May your Spirit flow, through us, all around us, below, above, and within us. Ground our bodies, strengthen our souls, open our hearts to dance in praise of you, giver of life. Let us breathe in deeply, receiving "ruah" and breathe out slowly, releasing flowing love.

In movement meditation the sacred dancer demonstrates through her or his body a balance of action, awareness, and contemplation. The practice involves stillness and focused prayer combined with exercises opening to flowing movement and ecstatic response to scripture, nature, and the urgings of our life. A contemplative dimension to working allows the dancer to shift from *doing* the dance to *being* the dance.

I teach my students to develop an increasingly inclusive awareness of what is transpiring inside them as they dance. This awareness includes the interaction of physical, mental, emotional, and spiritual dimensions of their being. Awareness, coupled with detachment, underlies the dancer's ability to be centered throughout the movements. Surrendering all of one's self then becomes an offering.

Through the various forms of dance meditation we work toward becoming increasingly aware of God "within" and God "without." The sacred dancer, searching for God through the medium of dance, intuitively practices a double form of meditation: she is centered on the "still point" within her, and she becomes aware of what she is experiencing. For example, the dancer may begin moving with a strong sense of her heart centered in God. While holding this awareness, she may perceive her "center" as flowing throughout her body. Aware of this flow, she allows it to shape her body into myriad forms, creating rhythmic and dynamic fluctuations. Her movements, in turn, affect the space around her. She is one with all that is happening. Drawn by the beauty of this stream of movement, she is as a river flowing onward, giving "voice" to a song from within. Or she can become a tree, motionless except for leaves that shimmer and flutter, whispering as the Spirit moves. Drawing from the varied gifts of the world, or incarnate life around us, she even becomes like the Theotokos, the God-bearer whose "ecstasy will give birth to divine life."[3]

Breath and the Dancer

The bird sings, the dancer dances—dance and breath are natural partners; wind, breath, the living earth, and the dancing "body of

---

[3] Ibid., 163.

Christ" are in relationship. This is reminiscent of what Beatrice refers to as a "cosmic, incarnational mysticism."[4] For me, if God is incarnate, all of life is breathing and dancing.

The dancer, for stamina, learns to breathe fully and deeply, more or less consciously. Breath has a long, long past, beginning with the creation story in Genesis where God's breath is the gift of life, "while a wind from God swept over the face of the waters" (Gen 1:2). "Then the LORD God formed man from the dust of the ground, and breathed into his nostrils the breath of life; and the man became a living being" (Gen 2:7). And finally,

> For Wisdom is more mobile than any
>   motion; . . .
> she is a breath of the power of God.
>   (Wis 7:24–25)

Movement depends on our breath to sustain it. When we inhale, our chest expands, we are filled, we receive God's spirit with each breath. Exhaling, emptying, we contract, drawing inward. To illustrate in a visceral way the integral nature of breath and form, let's turn to how a lament might be danced, for example, the phrase "How long, O God?" For my purposes, the movement in this case begins as a formless sigh from deep within, and then releases into form. Breathing in and out, bent over, I pulse, as in sobbing. I then breathe in deeply for preparation, chest lifting and expanding. Then, breathing out, I utter the prayer silently, reaching with my arm extending upward while exhaling, creating a tension between sinking and reaching. This may be a dramatic description, but I think it illustrates the interrelatedness of body and soul; earth, air and spirit; the need for people to connect with God with their whole being through breath. And, if the dancer pauses, waiting upon the Spirit in wordless dialogue, suspended, listening to receive a response, we are nearing the "still point," a pivotal concept in dance and referred to in T. S. Eliot's classic poem "Burnt Norton":

---

[4] Ibid., 176.

Except for the point, the still point,
There would be no dance, and there is only
the dance.[5]

Aesthetics

An underlying factor shaping dance meditation is a quest for *beauty*. As movement begins to flow, a kinesthetic sense of beauty draws one's soul to follow the unfolding gift that is taking place. Urged by beauty, the dancer-meditator, passive, as a receptacle, but active as an instrument, accompanies the movement's journey toward its epiphany. God becomes identified with the journey, with consciousness, suffering, beauty, and discovery. The dancer, capable of moving from the depths to the heights of human emotion, may be aware of being carried by God's love.

It has been said that as the body loves exercise, so the soul loves awareness. Dance meditation happens generally with intention, whether during a dance sequence or a movement exercise devised to this end. Yet it may also begin as "dance prayer" and drop into stillness—a stillness that is alive, like silent reverberation after a struck bell. It is an experience of being lured by beauty. The arts have a divine capacity to make visible the invisible—to behold beauty and reveal it to others. Hence, beauty reveals the face of God. Together we give praise, forming an ecstatic community of awareness and interrelatedness. As Thomas Merton so wonderfully notes, "Yet the fact remains that we are invited to forget ourselves on purpose, cast our awful solemnity to the winds and join in the general dance."[6] This is integral to the dance of the Trinity. Right as we are, we are invited to catch echoes of the great dance, moving with or without intentional awareness, participating in a great communal dance of ecstatic unity.

---

[5] T. S. Eliot, "Burnt Norton," in *Four Quartets* (New York: Harcourt, Brace, and World, 1943), 15–16.

[6] Thomas Merton, *Choosing to Love the World: On Contemplation*, ed. Jonathan Montaldo (Boulder, CO: Sounds True, 2008), 42.

Throughout my work as a sacred dancer I have found myself questioning the distinction between sacred and secular. I am asking this now to gain insight into how dance may be part of an evolutionary thrust of the universe, which leads me to want to explore what it is that makes a dance sacred. Is it the dancer's intention or method of creating that makes a dance sacred? Is it the dance's function in a community? Is it a gift or a grace bestowed by God? Perhaps it is being in touch with that which is larger than one's self that brings about a transcendent dimension, all the while honoring the wisdom of the body.

In the ancient period, dance had a profound and essential role in humanity's sense of God, foundational to and permeating all aspects of community life. Gerardus van der Leeuw, writing about the loss of unity between dance and religion, considers much of dance as pure entertainment, "a fossil of the living dance, which once had its own, much more inclusive, social function." But he also sees dance by its very nature as religious, when dance is the natural expression of the person "who is just as conscious of his body as he is of his soul. In the dance, the boundaries of the body and soul are effaced. The body moves itself spiritually, the spirit bodily."[7] This is a helpful breakdown as we seek to mend the split between body and soul in our spirituality and as we seek healing for our times.

Propelled by God's Love: The Gift of Hope

I believe underlying the desire to be healed and to dance is the gift of hope. We have to have hope to dance, and dance in turn is healing and gives substance to hope. When we dance, our spirits lift; what has become stagnant or buried within us has a chance to become unblocked and flow through us. Our moods begin to shift, what had been perceived as overwhelming dissipates as the healing process brings into the light what has been buried. Thus, we are more likely to be aware of and engage in new

---

[7] Gerardus van der Leeuw, *Sacred and Profane Beauty: The Holy in Art* (New York: Abingdon Press, 1963), 33, 35.

relationships with people, with the world, and with cares outside of our smaller worlds. Unexpected elements of the "divine milieu" emerge. Diversity within unity becomes less threatening and more thoroughly appreciated.

The Omega Point and the Still Point

I am drawn to weave together a connection, as I see it as a dancer, between Teilhard de Chardin's "Omega Point" (a forward thrust and convergence of Christic consciousness in and outside of time) and T. S. Eliot's famous "still point of the turning world."[8] A dancer who is moving deeper toward her innermost center through practice, meditation, improvisation, performance, prayer, community (and any number of special graces) is thus drawing nearer to everybody else's center. As her dance rises from her depth, she converges with all that also rises, meeting at the "still point of the turning world." Imagine the tremendous flow and energy of love that is released as dancers draw together, interacting with one another and the world by dancing with life; sharing hopes and sufferings; interlacing harmony, joy and peace. Beatrice's closing thoughts in *God's Ecstasy* are for us to "rejoice in the cosmos" and to be "active, and to contribute in artwork, healing, and understanding."[9] Wisdom sets the tone:

> I was daily his [God's] delight,
>   rejoicing before him always,
>   rejoicing in his inhabited world
>   and delighting in the human race.
>   (Prov 8:30–31)

If the whole world is the body of Christ (to make a leap connecting creatureliness, the cosmos, the dancer and the whole of humanity), then how we treat our body is how we treat the earth.

---

[8] Eliot, "Burnt Norton."
[9] Bruteau, *God's Ecstacy*, 179.

As we breathe, the earth breathes (when we keep it healthy), and the body of Christ dances. The earth, blessed, rejoices with her inhabitants as they rejoice in her. Is not God in our midst, dancing with timbrel and drum? Are we not "co-creating" with God? The psalms give us vivid descriptions of how dancing speaks in gestures of thanks and praise:

> You have turned my mourning into dancing.
> (Ps 30:11)

And, so beautifully,

> Let them praise his name with dancing,
>   making melody with timbrel and lyre.
> (Ps 149:3)

Perichoresis

The inner journey of the sacred dancer is coupled with insights garnered from the practice of dance meditation. Beatrice's spirit-filled sense of hope and evolutionary outlook on the universe urged me to reflect on the role of dance in our incarnational, cosmic, and mystical theology. This is developed through the concept of perichoresis or dance of the Trinity.

What might be a dancer's depiction of the dance of the Trinity? We are dancing with God, in God's presence everywhere, with Jesus, in the fullness of love, inflamed by the Holy Spirit. We are called children of God, and have eyes to see, and a new heart and mind to comprehend what is being revealed. God is not only my partner in this dance, but I am part of God's dance. What does the indwelling, completely living, dynamic trinitarian relationships of Father, Son, and Holy Spirit look like as the Trinity dances in our midst, embracing the whole world in love? Diana Wear, Bay Area homilist, recently preached on Trinity Sunday, incorporating this notion of perichoresis and engaging the assembly to live, move, and dance, with our trinitarian God:

Now let us ponder and move with an image of the Trinity. Picture God . . . loving justice and what is right, commanding and powerful in creating the heavens and earth, yet filled with kindness and being One in whom we place our hope. Envision Jesus, the one who is perhaps more human, whom we relate to as a person, a close friend who says at the end of today's gospel passage, "I am with you always." Recall those encounters in the stories we've heard from gospel accounts and how we want to emulate that justice-seeking, compassionate friend. Third, imagine the Holy Spirit, who moves in and among us, helps us to grow, change, and develop as better Christians and filled with faith—both individually as well as communally. Living trinitarian faith means living *from* and *for* our magnificent, all-merciful God, living *with* and *for* others, as Jesus taught and did, and trusting in a Spirit that *moves throughout* our bodies, our communities, and our world.[10]

Then she added movement from my own corpus of dance instruction, encouraging the congregation to dance with the trinitarian image, using the circle dance to illustrate the Trinity in motion. "DeSola invites us to 'lift our arms, touch one another, gaze into each other's eyes, be in movement, and experience the Holy Spirit as it lives and moves in and through us.'" She ended her sermon with a question: "How do you dance with the three-person'd God?" To which I heartily respond, "by opening your arms and dancing!"

And yet we must be mindful also of the great dance of suffering revealed by Jesus. There is a dance that gathers the poor, the persecuted, and the desperate. The Beatitudes, as Jesus proclaimed, reveal a dance seemingly contradictory, but pointing to the mystery of time and eternity:

---

[10] Diana Wear, homily (May 31, 2015), paraphrasing Catherine Mowry LaCugna, *God with Us: The Trinity and Christian Life* (San Francisco: HarperSanFrancisco, 1991), 400.

"Blessed are you who are poor,
  for yours is the kingdom of God."
    (Luke 6:20)

Jesus concludes with the assurance of rejoicing.

Two more examples follow that I believe illustrate well this vision of dance and perichoresis. The first comes from a dance at a memorial service, and the second is dance enfolded into the eucharistic celebration.

I vividly recall the memorial service for Professor Doug Adams at the Pacific School of Religion in 2005. Before he died, Doug had asked me to choreograph various parts of his memorial liturgy, including inviting people into the church. He had specifically discussed wanting a New Orleans–type jazz band. I directed the dancers to gather the people facing the church from an outdoor garden with a stately dance, ringing Tibetan bowls. But then, unplanned and not choreographed, after everyone entered the sanctuary, to my amazement couples started dancing in the aisles to the jazz music! It was a spontaneous expression of how they remembered and celebrated Doug. It was a joy-filled dance. The Spirit was moving through their bodies, through the sanctuary, and among the community.

The second example took place in San Francisco, where St. Gregory of Nyssa Episcopal Church is often referred to as a dancing church. St. Gregory's has a panoply of modern icons depicting dancing saints, led by Jesus, their "dancing" leader. The colorful icons are painted near life size, high above in the rotunda in the sanctuary, one after another in a circle, beginning with Sojourner Truth and including Saint Francis and even a dancing bear! As a former rector explained, the vortex of their energy seems to hold up the roof.[11] Every Sunday, for the closing ritual at the end of mass, people form a circle around the altar (in the center of the rotunda) and, with singing and drumming, dance around the altar under the circle of dancing saints. Movement is

---

[11] Personal communication, Donald Schell, co-founder and former rector, St. Gregory of Nyssa Episcopal Church, June 14, 2015.

an integral part of their liturgy. The congregants process to the altar with a medieval dance step after the Liturgy of the Word; the passing of the consecrated bread and wine throughout the congregation is sacred movement, as is sharing in an extended peace greeting. This is reminiscent of the perichoresis referred to earlier in the homily on Trinity Sunday, and this congregation dances it every week!

Approaching Perichoresis

Circle dances have long endured. Images of the ring dance of the angels in medieval and Renaissance paintings like centuries of religious imagination. What follows is not quite a dance of that stateliness but rather a series of movement directions for groups that I call "In Honor of Perichoresis." Foundational aspects of this vision include giving and receiving, reverence for all, dancing with creation, an awareness of the dimension of suffering in the world, meditation, and stillness. Embedded within the dance should be the opportunity for ecstatic, improvisatory movement, thrusting the dancers into new patterns and dimensions of discovery. The dance should be both simple in structure so all can participate and beautifully improvised or choreographed to express our human/divine expression.

Preparation:

Music is critical and will shape the feeling of the dance and give life and inspiration to the participants. Good musical choices might include meditative chants or tunes that evolve into an ecstatic dimension, or better yet, live music with a flutist or drummer inviting people to dance.

The music begins and those assembled come into the center space and form a circle. The leader asks the participants to relax their hands and just stand there, consciously aware of their feet on the ground, their bodies alert but relaxed, letting go of any tensions, focused on breathing and awareness of God's presence in their bodies.

Directions for the Leader:

1. Look around the group and smile, appreciating everyone's presence. Bring your hands together in the traditional prayer position. Say: Let us *bow* to God and one another. *Pause.*

2. Say: Let us take hands and begin *walking* to our right (counter-clockwise) in the circle.

3. After a few steps let go of the hand of the person on your right and lead the dancers into a *spiral*.

4. The spiral winds in, almost to the center, at which point, turning to your right, you begin to unwind the circle. As people unwind they find themselves facing people still coming into the spiral, giving everyone the opportunity to see each of the others as they pass by.

5. As you reach the last person in the circle, turn to your left, beginning the process of creating the circle again, ending up with everyone facing toward the center.

6. Instruct the dancers to move to the center, raising their arms together, and then back out again.

> *Optional:* One person comes to the center, dancing as the inner flame of the gathering, as the Christ figure proclaiming the yearnings of humanity and the whole cosmos on its journey to God. As the soloist dances, the group gathers more and more closely. The dancer has lifted one arm up high in the center, like a beacon that draws together everyone's aspirations. The music fades or ends. *Pause.*

7. Invite all the participants to break from the circle and explore with their bodies the space around them, beginning

close to themselves, then spreading and moving far out, and then ending closer and closer together. During this time, you may call out specific words to help give direction or focus, such as:

> reach out toward the heavens
>
> reach low toward the ground
>
> reach all around
>
> explore the whole space, moving toward one another and away from one another
>
> explore the space rising, falling, circling, taking hands, following one another's movements (as in a mirror exercise)

8. Say: Select a new partner and dance together. Change partners.

9. Say: Now dance in groups of three or four people. Instruct the dancers to move with their group to the farthest reaches of the room.

10. Invite everyone to return to the center of the space, forming one group, like a *sculpture*. Bodies may touch one another but at different levels, closer or further away. Tell them to hold their position as the music stops. A new creation has been formed—Perichoresis at Play.

✳

Thanks and Farewell, Beatrice

For likening God to the dancer, and encouraging dance in my spiritual life.

For introducing me to Teilhard de Chardin's thoughts, thus inspiring me to name my dance company Omega Liturgical Dance Company, aiming to embody his hope and inner fire.

For enkindling in me a desire to meditate, after observing you in deep stillness during a conference at the Abbey of Gethsemani.

For enabling me to welcome insights from many different religious sources without fear, passed on by your own explorations of Eastern religions and East-West dialogue.

For your open and optimistic spirit, typified by how you would invariably greet a new guest inquiring: "Howdya do? And what have you done today to save the world?" I would laugh at the audaciousness of it, but I would have responded, "I danced for peace!"

Let us go with God, dancing . . .

11

My Journey with Beatrice

Joshua Tysinger

Beatrice came into my life unexpectedly. At a time in my life when I had been softening to the prospect of intensive spiritual direction, my wonderful mentor Rev. Cynthia Bourgeault dropped a priceless opportunity squarely upon my lap. I will never forget that life-altering day in March 2014 when Rev. Bourgeault graciously slipped me an arbitrary string of numbers via email, politely informing me that all those digits in what otherwise appeared to be an ordinary numerical sequence somehow added up to produce the telephone information of Dr. Beatrice Bruteau.

Having previously read her book *God's Ecstasy*, I was relatively familiar with Beatrice's musings on evolutionary consciousness. Her work expanded the ideas of the great Roman Catholic theologian and paleontologist Pierre Teilhard de Chardin, whose name at the time I could barely pronounce; Beatrice would later let me know it. To say the very least I was perpetually blown away, amazed and mesmerized by the intricacies of her thought. Yet in that moment, what I knew most tangibly was that here was a once in a lifetime opportunity to meet one of the most prodigious interspiritual scholars of our era, an unsung hero of twentieth century contemplative philosophy.

This momentous realization dawned upon me with all the force of a two-ton brick as I began evaluating the very real and weighty implications of making her acquaintance. As I painstakingly weighed both the pros and cons of pursuing this contact, one fearful question spontaneously arose: what if Beatrice took an intellectual hacksaw to my valued spiritual convictions? After all, who was I to approach a world-renowned religious scholar? As earnestly as the first thought entered into my awareness, another disheartening possibility demanded my attention: what if Beatrice brutally dismissed me as some kind of New Age hack or covert spiritual huckster? These were serious questions, demanding real-time answers and delicate consideration. After a few minutes of quiet deliberation, an inward voice popped up that said, "To hell with it!" and I called her two days later.

Now, as first conversations go, my introduction to Beatrice was a real doozy—an experience that remains forever lodged in my memory. En route to my apartment from Wake Forest School of Divinity in Winston-Salem, North Carolina, on a sunny spring day when I was currently rounding out the second semester of my first year of seminary studies, I picked up my cell phone and dialed the number Rev. Bourgeault had given me. After three rings had droned monotonously across my eardrum, a raspy voice answered with a resounding "hello?" I immediately responded with an initial presentation of name, the person who had referred me, and an awkward exchange of introductory pleasantries before preemptively cutting to the chase. Explaining to Beatrice that I had found myself attending seminary in her own backyard, after having been attracted to her ideas for quite sometime, I revealed my own motivation to pursue her for provisional spiritual direction. As she quietly absorbed my not-so-subtle proposal, Beatrice replied, "Well, I don't know. Spiritual direction, you say? I haven't taken on students in quite some time and, in any case, I don't believe I'm the right person for you now. Besides, you must be pretty well learned at this point in your seminary education. Let me ask you one question: do you *believe* everything they're teaching you in school?" Taken aback by the directness of her question, I took a brief moment before formulating an answer.

What, in fact, had I learned over my past year in seminary? Had my experience boiled down to the rote memorization of theological jargon, critically analyzing speculative truth-claims *about* God for acceptable letters? Had I come even remotely close to approaching God, or was I simply spinning my wheels? Rather than delivering some half-baked response concocted from an academically correct script, I drew in a long, exhaustive breath and confessed my conviction in the power of the Eucharist. Before I could draw forth a coherent stream of words that might justify my position, Beatrice interrupted: "All right. Well, here's an idea. What *if* the Eucharist went beyond mere symbolism? Now let's suppose that you start out with the Holy Trinity as a simple proposition: that a plurality of persons can and do perform concrete tasks, all the time, in service of each other. Of course you have the Father, the Son, and the Holy Spirit all working together as free agents, collaboratively feeding into the Oneness of communion. When one dynamic person sends nourishment to other dynamic persons, it creates a process of sending and receiving. And within this dynamic give and take system, survival on spiritual food alone simply will not do. In order to keep the program running, you actually have to feed *all* the people for everything to work! Instead of administering a sip of wine and a wafer to get our point across, what do you think about setting up an actual banquet? One with real food?" In that moment, I knew with unshakable certainty that this brilliant woman had incarnated her version of the Holy Trinity. This mysterious agape-based principle was fully alive and well, operating in and vibrating throughout Beatrice's physical person. From my humble perspective, Beatrice was in the midst of actualizing the sum of her enviable life's works, and as a result I eagerly desired to know her.

After mining the complexities of the Eucharist for another forty-five minutes, I found myself delightfully locked into a formal lunchtime "meet and greet" the following day with Beatrice and her loving husband, Jim. Around noontime the very next day, I promptly arrived at an unassuming apartment, casually making my way toward a semi-open doorway. I could see two cats sprawled lazily on the patio. Knocking on what I recognized to be Beatrice's place of residence, it was only a matter of time before a petite woman appeared before the door. "Hello? Can I help you?" Reintroducing myself as Joshua, the Wake Forest School of Divinity student she had chatted with briefly the day before, I casually reminded her of our impending lunch arrangement. Seemingly caught off guard by a lack of recollection, Beatrice quipped back, "Well, now. A seminary student? I see. We're already saved in this house—but if you happen to have a decent proposal for our time and attention, we might just hear you out." At that precise moment, a pang of recognition swept across my body. How surreal was this sensation, I thought, given the idiosyncratic nature of our exchange? And yet, it seemed to me as if this exact moment had played out several times prior, eerily echoing an analogously playful tone. Had Beatrice and I met before? Was this déjà vu? After retreating into the living room for a brief consultation with Jim—who was lounging comfortably on the couch—Beatrice's booming voice suddenly burst forth, "Come on in, stranger! Let's get acquainted and then how about some lunch?"

Adventures with Beatrice

From that day forward I found myself conforming to a regularly scheduled series of set meetings at K&W Cafeterias with my newfound pedagogue, Beatrice. Little did I know at the time that those meetings would persist over the next four months. At a rate of three to four times a week, I drove to Beatrice's apartment for a brief "how do you do?" before we eventually loped off to her favorite eatery. While our conversations at K&W Cafeterias typically ranged from theology to developmental psychology and quantum physics, the real depth contained within our wonderful encounters naturally arose from an intersubjective space. Because her teachings rapidly unfurled through shared dialogue and deep relational bonding, never once did I feel inferior, intimidated, or patronized by the nature of her methods. Beatrice artfully combined systematic inquiry with her signature blend of intelligence, insight, and wisdom to expand my consciousness incrementally over the course of our outings. As a matter of fact, most of her teachings sank into my awareness subtly during what might have otherwise been construed as normal dialogue. Still, on a few occasions it occurred to me that something special was happening.

At the ripe old age of eighty-three, Beatrice struggled with dementia; however, she seemed to inhabit an extraordinary space that went beyond cognition. Having so thoroughly transcended the heavy burdens of separateness and division, it was no mystery to me, nor did it really matter, that Beatrice maneuvered around my "psychic grid" with unlimited access. And while I cannot recall the specific moment when she dwelled deeply inside my heart—her resplendent presence residing there alongside her supportive husband, Jim—the undeniable transfusion of energies between us was so powerful that I could have conceived of nothing different.

What in K&W Cafeterias did Beatrice find so appealing? The wholesome family atmosphere of K&W Cafeterias provided countless opportunities to whet her insatiable social urges. It was almost as if the eucharistic dimension of Beatrice's teachings livened through the time-honored pattern of dining and mingling. The employees at K&W Cafeterias often referred to Beatrice by name and would frequently approach our table for a handshake or a hug. On any given day she might manically dart toward whichever stranger crossed her path, doling out loads of compliments and generous affection.

On one occasion Beatrice mercilessly tracked down a bystander as she strolled innocently toward the exit. As I peered on in distress, the woman, who by that time had been placed into a bear hug by Beatrice, softly asked me, "Honey, why do you look so embarrassed? Why, if we had more Christians like this remarkable woman, could you imagine what the world would be like?" Perhaps this lady knew something that I certainly did not. According to Beatrice, "What genuinely sustains people is positive encouragement. Why, everyone deserves praise from time to time. . . . Don't you?" This sentiment couldn't have been closer to the truth, for those patrons having been fortunate enough to receive her loving hugs and kindness rarely left dissatisfied.

Once when I asked Beatrice about her preference for eating at K&W Cafeterias, she turned toward me with a dignified, matronly look and exclaimed, "For the children, of course! So many children lack proper care and nurturance. Now, stop for just one moment and take a look around. There are children as far as the eye can see!" In any event, over the course of our adventures at K&W Cafeterias, I never once questioned the fact that Beatrice was its mother, and all its patrons were her children.

Now, on many occasions my beautiful fiancée, Helena Epstein, accompanied us on our outings, helping Beatrice with the grueling task of picking out her meals. One afternoon when Helena was not present, however, we hit the food line, where a copious assortment of salads, appetizers, entrees, and desserts were laid out. When we finally approached the check out, Beatrice's eyes lit up. Her ever-so-excited brow began to furrow, and she turned toward me and asked, "How old are you?" Oh, no. Here we go again. I panicked. Hadn't we covered this base already nearly two dozen times this week? Her inquiry led me to suspect that we were about to embark upon a highly sensitive and redundant subject that I desperately desired to avoid. Privately wincing, I slowly arched my back before sucking in some air, expelled a long breath, and replied: thirty. Of course, this verbal response prompted the necessary and sufficient tie-in that illustrated Beatrice's point, "Better get going, fellow! If you want to have children, now's the time! You better get to it!" The various implications of feeding into this unforgiving thought-cycle were precarious and harrowing, as I very well knew. After all, by the time you took note of Beatrice careening down this rabbit hole, it became impossible to pull her out. "Well, what's your position? Time's a' wasting!" she prodded as we strolled toward the table where Jim patiently waited.

As I dropped my tray and silverware down upon the mahogany-colored surface, I pondered whether or not it would be more practical just to let this one go. If I responded that Helena and I were waiting until we eventually settled down into our prospective Episcopal vocations, Beatrice would have a field day. And yet, if I played my cards just right, perhaps allowing her to take the torch and run with it, consenting to having children sooner rather than later, maybe, just maybe, she would graciously let me off the hook.

Articulating the precise words that Beatrice longed to hear, I responded that Helena and I were about to hop aboard the baby-making train sometime very soon. How would Beatrice respond? Would she divert her attention elsewhere, or was I now helplessly hemmed into this disingenuous conversation about childrearing? Beatrice piped back, "Very good! Wise decision, if I say so myself. You won't be sorry."

I knew that Beatrice's major life regret was not having children. Perhaps the potency of Beatrice's teaching style could be attributed to this significant fact alone, since her maternal hardwiring had been sublimated to such a remarkable degree that the whole world became her family. "Jim! Can you hear me?" Beatrice bellowed abruptly, as she elbowed her ninety-eight-year-old partner in the rib cage, "Are we too old to adopt?" As Jim momentarily glanced up, Beatrice continued, "Can you hear me, Jim? What do you think about adoption?"

Never one to shy away from inserting his unique brand of dry humor, Jim replied, "I don't have any thoughts, Beatrice. You know I'm a Buddhist!"

Clearly exasperated, Beatrice rebutted, "Well that's the most ridiculous thing I've ever heard. We all know that Buddhists have thoughts too!"

Peering back to where I sat at the other end of the table, Beatrice proceeded, "As I was just about to mention, what's important for you to learn is how to properly hold a child. First of all, you have to assume that it's been decently fed and nourished. Then you have to approach the infant ever so gently and curl your palm behind its neck." And with that, Beatrice got up, shoved her chair in, and made her way to my end of the table. Swiftly cupping the back of my head and placing her palm upon my heart, she cradled me over and over again for the next five minutes, intermittently uttering, "Goo, goo, goo!" As this florid demonstration of ideal parental attunement unfolded before Jim, whose eyes reflected unprecedented shock, Beatrice descended into the sweet maternal rhythms of unified bliss. "Goo, goo, goo!"

Five minutes later, after I had been lulled into a state of tranquil nonresistance, Beatrice had had her fill from me. She suddenly leapt up and launched herself into an adjacent booth for another hearty helping. The parents of the infant Beatrice was now nurturing could not have resisted this fairy godmother, even if they had tried. As Beatrice rocked the child back and forth, I couldn't help but wonder: was Beatrice modeling God?

The Tipping Point

Toward the end of July, we celebrated Beatrice's eighty-fourth birthday with a cake, a card, a plush white bear, and a lovely white orchid marked by purple and yellow spots to complement her other bevy of flowers. Since Beatrice and Jim had already prepared a few prepackaged dinners prior to our arrival, Helena and I were content to celebrate the afternoon by basking in their company. Over the next two hours we casually bantered, exchanged jokes, and merrily blew out candles, after which Beatrice endearingly snuggled her bear. Although things were going exceedingly well, these good vibrations, however strong they were, were not meant to last.

Within a few days Beatrice had fractured her hip. This tragedy occurred one fateful afternoon while Beatrice was attending to her cats. Near the patio of her apartment she lost her balance, slipped, and fell hard onto the grass. She was soon whisked away to the local hospital, where she received immediate medical care. Over the next week Beatrice remained confined to her bland and sanitary hospital room despite her best intentions to return to the comfortable and unsupervised privacy of her apartment. Her always fierce sense of self-determination combined with the circular pattern of dementia to produce never-ending spirals of, "When can I go home?" or "How did this happen?" and "I know my rights, and they're keeping me here against my will!" On one occasion, when confronted by her case manager about plans for rehabilitation, Beatrice snapped back: "So you're suggesting to me that I undergo a program where someone stays with me at night, and yet you're asking me to stay apart from Jim? It seems to me that you're in the business of separating families!" Of course, Beatrice's perceptions were exaggerated by the nature of her condition. However, they were not without merit. Because the severity of her hip fracture prevented stable ambulation, for the foreseeable future Beatrice would become increasingly dependent on the help of her aides.

The following week Beatrice and Jim were transported to a nearby rehabilitation center for continued medical support. During this period one of Rev. Cynthia Bourgeault's students, Dr. Rudolph Hwa, a renowned particle physicist and professor from the University of Oregon, arrived in town on a pilgrimage to meet Beatrice. Spanning a magnificent two-day period of teaching and transmission, Beatrice would arise—from what she might later refer to as her period of "indolent slumber"—to impart fiery discourses on mathematics, wisdom, and the Holy Trinity. This impromptu pedagogical whirlwind was motivated in part by the presence of Dr. Hwa, whose venerable mastery in the fields of physics and mathematics inspired a sweeping philosophical discourse. On day two of his visit, after Dr. Hwa and Beatrice had launched into an intense conversation about the theoretical sciences, a beautiful dialogue suddenly emerged:

Rudolph: Mathematics is pure logic, and yet I find it very difficult to relate mathematics to the world.

Beatrice: When you try, how does it come out?

Rudolph: It's a tool, for me.

Beatrice: Yes, but you can abstract the tool and make a system from it. The wonderful thing about mathematics—which we've either invented, or discovered, if you prefer—is that we can use it to understand the real world, the world that's going to be the way it is whether you like it or not. But the one you make up when you're doing pure mathematics is the one you've fallen in love with.

Joshua: When I look at the Holy Trinity and examine the one, the two, and the three, each character seems to have an assigned value of meaning but only interdependently and in relation to the other. No number can stand alone, can it?

Beatrice: What you put down in your givens will then govern the rest of your construction.

Joshua: And yet, there must be an ontological internalization of the meaning systems assigned to numerical values for all of it to make sense, correct?

Beatrice: If you're also going to believe it about yourself and the world that you observe, you have to play by the rules. . . .

Joshua: And yet, we're also self-creating. So we can at times bend the rules of the system?

Beatrice: Yes, but that just means you're adding another rule to the system.

Joshua: Where do you believe that wisdom comes from?

Beatrice: You! If by wisdom you mean the reliability of propositions about the world, then you're the one who makes the propositions. Of course, when you look at the world, ultimately you're going to have to determine which type of views you're going to allow into your system. If you take a view and put it in your system, a view that contradicts other views you've already accepted, then it really will not work. A person with wisdom should have complete freedom within that world, where the propositions are consistent with one another and without contradiction. But then that person has to find out whether or not they are complete. With the world, we try to make a propositional schema for wisdom, and yet sometimes we get kind of stuck or hung up with contradictions because it isn't quite the one the world is doing it by. People think that they discover wisdom, and maybe in some ways they do, but they also make it up. And somebody might say, "By gosh, is that how God makes the world? Well! That's a nice question." . . .

Rudolph: Which number is of more interest to you—three or seven?

Beatrice: Three, partly because it's smaller. And so it has more application.

Joshua: Rev. Cynthia Bourgeault places a large emphasis on the numbers three and seven. According to her, the law of three and the law of seven . . .

Beatrice (chuckling): What does she think about the number thirteen?

Rudolph: If you notice, all three numbers you mentioned are prime numbers.

Beatrice (chuckling): Well, they're all odd numbers, to say the least. And they're all primes. . . . The thing about prime numbers is that there are an infinite number of them.

Rudolph: I once counted the number of spokes on a spider web.

Beatrice: Are they always primes?

Rudolph: I found it to be seventeen. Before that time, I believed that a spider web would be so symmetrical that it could not produce a prime number. I have been fascinated by spiders ever since.

Beatrice: Do you think that prime-ness has anything to do with creating a new species?

Rudolph: No, I was not thinking so much as I was marveling.

Beatrice: Well, the world is there to be marveled at. What do you think?

Helena: I'm still thinking about the number three.

Beatrice: What do you think of three?

Helena: I was actually just thinking about what you wrote in *God's Ecstasy* about the number three. Three is the smallest quantity necessary for creating community, and once you have more than two, then you start getting into a dynamic interplay that is truly reliant on creativity, interdependence, and mutual responses for development and survival.

Beatrice (chuckling): Gee, that's interesting. You should write about it.

Helena: You did!

Rudolph: You also said that agape could only come into life with at least three members.

Beatrice: What would you say?

Helena: I tend to think of relationship in terms of two, but since I've been reflecting on the process of three, it's helpful to begin removing the conceptual barriers of relationship in order to expand it out naturally. . . .

Beatrice: Does God get mixed up in this sort of thing?

Helena: I think that God is at the bottom of the whole thing.

Rudolph: Let me remind you of what you wrote about three. You see, if I love Josh and he loves me, but he also loves Helena, then I must also love Helena. . . .

Beatrice: If you want to be able to hold this thing together within certain limited bounds, then you have to get your original propositions just right so that they'll enable you to do that.

Joshua: Such as, if I love you, then I must also love Jim, because you love Jim. It's a chain. . . .

Beatrice: Yes! How much can you apply that to, let's say, the world?

Joshua: Oh, gosh! It goes on infinitely.

Beatrice: This world, if it's going to hold together, has to be consistent with itself.

Joshua: I was wondering, what is the hallmark of being a good teacher?

Beatrice: Excitement. And I think that it should be exciting stuff that you tell people about. It shouldn't be dull. And that the pupils should be capable of getting excited about it, otherwise they're just not mathematicians. Mathematics is a creative world, not a found world, like botany. And somebody might step up and say, "Have you ever studied much botany? It's full of insight and limitation, and this thing that entails that thing. Creatures have to live by logic just like anybody else."

Joshua: I'd like to be a teacher someday and was wondering what advice you might give someone like me?

Beatrice: Do you know what subject you'd want to teach?

Joshua: I'd like to help people do the kind of inner work necessary to be more loving and self-satisfied. . . .

Beatrice: Do you think that it helps students to get organized by doing things logically?

Joshua: I believe logic plays a big part in that.

Beatrice: But I think a lot of people who are into the mystical thing eschew logic. I think that they're mistaken, but that doesn't mean that we don't have to take it into consideration. Because if they think that the kind of relationship they're having with God is independent from the kind of mathematics they're doing it by, then you've got to look into that.

Rudolph: Would you say some more about mysticism?

Beatrice: First, you have to decide what your definition of mysticism is going to be. And then you have to ask what are the conditions necessary to make mysticism possible.

Joshua: So you're saying that mysticism is an individual-specific experience and it's kind of important to define that for one's self?

Beatrice: You could say that. But if you're in a community situation you have to say up front, "By mysticism I shall mean the following . . . "

Joshua: I'd say that mysticism perhaps is that part of tradition that bypasses dogma and gets into the foundational experience encountered by the early church visionaries.

Beatrice: Can mysticism be anything other than experience? Can you have somebody that lays down the law by what you describe as mysticism? Or is mysticism the fundamental experience of its kind that exists at the very beginning? Mysticism is not a conclusion. It's an origin.

Did Beatrice encounter this origin as an ontological fact? Was the consciousness of God so inextricably interwoven into Beatrice's experience that she encountered union with the source and object of our questions? While I remain reticent to over-spiritualize what Beatrice knew or did not, there was no doubt among Helena, Rudolph, and myself that this woman had gone beyond ordinary awareness. In hindsight, the content of her teachings were less significant than the presence she maintained, the energy she emitted, and the way in which she spoke to every one of us as if to the origins of our being. It was apparent to me then that her wisdom was being transferred, yet it was not immediately clear why or what was happening. At that crucial point in Beatrice's life process, Rudolph's very presence seemed to activate a tipping point in her evolutionary development—one that unleashed a fragrant outpouring of energies as she approached her final chapter. A new phase of her existence finally took form.

The Ascent

By mid-August, Beatrice was discharged and transported back to her apartment. From then on, she would be graced by medical in-home support. Since Beatrice was not able to walk up the stairs that led to her second-floor bedroom, her bed was relocated to the first-floor dining area, where it remained until the end. In mid-September, Beatrice was once again admitted to the hospital with a minor gastrointestinal inflammation. While on the surface this malady appeared to be nonthreatening, what remained truly disconcerting was that her weight had plummeted to approximately seventy pounds. Although she was never a heavy eater, Beatrice now refused her meals and relied on a steady diet of liquids and ice cream. During this time Beatrice and I routinely discussed her dissatisfaction with her litany of physical ailments as well as the subsequent constraints that had been imposed upon her freedom. What had become increasingly bothersome, from

Beatrice's perspective, was that the recent rash of illnesses and the dementia that plagued her mind were inevitably there to stay.

What began as a treatable gastrointestinal condition, within the blink of an eye turned into a contagious bacterial infection. Sometime after returning home Beatrice was placed in solitary seclusion. As a result, her friends were urged either to stay away or to approach her with tender care and caution. Her weight continued to drop at a rate that was both painful and alarming to watch. Beatrice gradually took to her bed. She refused to eat. Despite the opposition of her helpers, there was never a question as to who was really in charge. By late October palliative care was called in to navigate the final stages of her journey. At this critical juncture Beatrice slipped into the softer realms of sleep, awakening only for the company of guests. During this time she wisely encouraged me to summon her beloved goddaughter, Carla DeSola, so that we could mutually collaborate on planning her funeral. When Carla made her visit, traveling from Berkeley, California, Beatrice suddenly bounced back with enormous passion and vigor. Her energy was crisp, pure, and vibrant, resounding with the powerful authority of a woman who was moving closer to the edge.

After Carla left, nothing but silence lingered. On some afternoons immediately following school, I drove over to Beatrice and Jim's apartment just to sit beside her, to hold her hand, and to close my eyes in hopes of absorbing her presence. Throughout this period I remained keenly aware of just how much she had blessed me. With each precious and fragile breath, her radial essence never ceased to illuminate my inmost core as I sat and waited. One day, after Beatrice had awakened, I informed her about the powerful sensation of déjà vu that I had experienced the first time we met. Afterward, I asked her if it was possible that we had previously known each other, perhaps in another incarnation. Beatrice beamed ever so brightly. "That makes me feel very comforted, Josh," she said as she rolled back into her pillow.

Our conversation then turned toward discussing her biggest life regret: that she never bore children. "At least we've produced a successful offspring in you," she commented, as her eyes pierced mine. "There are those who *have to be* and those who *can be*, Josh. Knowing those who *can be* comes with the necessity of *having to be*. When you become aware that you *have to be*, your defenses will drop. The need will no longer exist to identify and make your position known. Those who *have to be* continuously return for a reason—because they *have to be*, they possess a similar purpose with those *coming into being*." Wow! OK, I'm following. "Now, let me ask you: does light need light, Josh?" Why yes, dear Beatrice. Yes, it most certainly does. One wick needs the flame of another in order to bring its light to existence. "That's right. Most theologies about God are really just musings about one's own condition. In life, the one true thing that matters is lending others your awareness. Now, if you'd like to be of service, you can clip my nails before you leave." And on one of my final visits with the great Dr. Beatrice Bruteau, I clipped away at her fingernails with all the giddiness of a child.

Later that November, Beatrice arose from her bed, shrugged off her lethargy, and regained the ability to walk. To say the least, this surprising new twist stunned everyone involved, and I was certainly no exception. In no time at all we became convinced that she was embarking down a path that would lead to a miraculous improvement. Defying all odds, Beatrice confidently roamed around her apartment as if nothing had ever happened. Our optimism soared! Had a miracle occurred? Although each of us retained high hopes for an improbable recovery, I privately sensed that this was not to be.

On the evening of November 23, Beatrice and Jim eased upon their couch to watch *The Roosevelt's* on PBS. Prompted by the randomness of thought or perhaps a "sponsor a child" television commercial, Beatrice flew off onto her usual tangent of desiring to adopt children. Nevertheless, sometime after midnight, Beatrice soared quietly into the ether. While her final wish to be a mother typifies the kind of person she embodied, it also reflects what she continued to offer countless other people. In life, I considered Beatrice to be my beloved spiritual mother. In death, she continues to teach me from wherever she exists now. And if I remain fortunate enough, one day I'm sure we'll meet again out there—somewhere in the ether.

Contributors

Rev. Cynthia Bourgeault is an Episcopal priest, writer, and retreat leader. She is the founding director of the Aspen Wisdom School, a core faculty member of the Living School for Action and Contemplation, and a former fellow of the Collegeville Institute for Ecumenical Research in Collegeville, Minnesota. She is the author of eight books, including *The Holy Trinity and the Law of Three*, *The Wisdom Jesus*, *The Wisdom Way of Knowing*, and *Centering Prayer and Inner Awakening*.

Ilia Delio, OSF, holds the Josephine C. Connelly Endowed Chair in Theology at Villanova University. She has a doctorate in pharmacology from Rutgers University-Healthcare and Biomedical Sciences and a doctorate in historical theology from Fordham University. She is the author of sixteen books, including *The Unbearable Wholeness of Being: God, Evolution and the Power of Love,* which won a book award from the Catholic Press Association and a Silver Nautilus Book Award; and *From Teilhard to Omega: CoCreating an Unfinished Universe.* Her latest book, *Making All Things New: Catholicity, Cosmology, and Consciousness,* initiates a new series, Catholicity in an Evolving Universe, published by Orbis Books.

Carla DeSola is a sacred dancer, choreography, teacher, and author. She founded the Omega Liturgical Dance Company at St. John the Divine Cathedral in New York City and Omega West in the San Francisco Bay area. Carla holds a diploma from Juilliard, and an MA from the Pacific School of Religion. She teaches courses at the Graduate Theological Union, Berkeley, through the Center for the Arts, Religion, and Education

Kathleen Duffy, SSJ, is professor of physics at Chestnut Hill College, where she directs the Interdisciplinary Honors Program and the Institute for Religion and Science. She is editor of *Teilhard Studies* and serves on the advisory boards of the American Teilhard Association and Cosmos and Creation. Her present research explores how Teilhard de Chardin's religious writings connect with modern science. She has published several book chapters and articles on these topics, an edited volume of essays entitled *Rediscovering Teilhard's Fire,* and *Teilhard's Mysticism: Seeing the Inner Face of Evolution.*

Barbara Fiand, SNDdeN, is a retired professor of philosophical and spiritual theology and the author of ten books. She lectures and gives retreats and workshops throughout the country and abroad on issues related to holistic spirituality, human matura-tion, prayer, the influence of quantum discoveries on spirituality, and the transformation of consciousness.

Kerrie Hide is a theologian and spiritual director. She has written many articles on mystical theology, prayer, and spirituality and is the author of the award-winning *Gifted Origins to Graced Fulfilment: The Soteriology of Julian of Norwich.* After eighteen years lecturing in the school of theology at Australian Catholic University and nine years as a spiritual director at St Mary's Towers, Douglas Park, she continues to enjoy doing spiritual direction, retreat work, and writing.

Ursula King is professor emerita of theology and religious studies and senior research fellow at the Institute for Advanced Studies, University of Bristol, England. Educated in Germany, France, India, and England—she earned the STL in Paris, MA in Delhi, and PhD in London—she has lectured all over the world and published widely on gender issues in religions, modern Hinduism, interfaith dialogue, spirituality, and Pierre Teilhard de Chardin, especially his biography *Spirit of Fire* and his selected spiritual writings in Orbis's Modern Spiritual Masters Series. She has held several visiting chairs in the United States and Norway and has been awarded honorary doctorates by the universities of Edinburgh, Oslo, and Dayton (Ohio).

John Shea is a theologian and storyteller who lectures nationally and internationally on faith-based healthcare, contemporary spirituality, storytelling in world religions, and the Spirit at Work movement. Currently, he is a senior fellow of the Ministry Leadership Center, which designs and implements formation programming for senior healthcare leaders of five West Coast Catholic healthcare systems.

Brie Stoner is a musician and recent graduate of the Living School for Action and Contemplation. Besides contributing to the Center for Spiritual Resources and Contemplative Wisdom blog, her work includes published records and production and composition of the soundtracks for the NOOMA series featuring Rob Bell. She is the mother of two young boys and lives in Grand Rapids, Michigan.

Joshua Tysinger is dedicated to works of social justice and interspirituality. He began his calling with several non-profit organizations serving the homeless in Asheville and Winston-Salem, North Carolina, and has since dedicated his time to issues of peace, equality, inter-systemic well-being, and nonviolent action.

The Works of Beatrice Bruteau

Books and Edited Volumes
Published in English and in Translation

1972   *Worthy Is the World: The Hindu Philosophy of Sri Aurobindo.* Rutherford: Fairleigh Dickinson University Press.

1975   *Evolution toward Divinity: Teilhard de Chardin and the Hindu Traditions.* Wheaton, IL: Quest Books.

                        Evolution Hacia La Divinidad [Spanish Translation, 1977].

1979   *The Psychic Grid: How We Create the Word We Know.* Wheaton, IL: Quest Books.

1990   *Silence in the Midst of Noise* [Edited Volume].

1991   *As We Are One: Essays and Poems in Honor of Bede Griffiths* [Edited Volume]. Pfafftown, NC: Philosopher's Exchange.

1993   *Radical Optimism: Rooting Ourselves in Reality.* New York: Crossroad.

1995   *What We Can Learn from the East.* New York: Crossroad.

                        Erlebst Du, Was Du Glaubst?: Was der Westen vom Osten Lernen Kann [German Translation, 1998].

1995   *The Easter Mysteries.* New York: Crossroad.

                        The Easter Mysteries [Reprint in Bandra, Mumbal, India, 1997].

1996   *The Other Half of My Soul: Bede Griffiths and the Hindu-Christian Dialogue* [Edited Volume]. Wheaton, IL: Quest Books.

1997	*God's Ecstasy: The Creation of a Self-Creating World.* New York: Crossroad.
2001	*The Grand Option: Personal Transformation and a New Creation.* Notre Dame, IN: University of Notre Dame Press.
	Jesus through Jewish Eyes: Rabbis and Scholars Engage an Ancient Brother in a New Conversation [Edited Volume]. Maryknoll, NY: Orbis Books.
	Jesus secundo o judaísmo: Rabinos estodiosos dealogam em nova perspective arespeito de um antigo irmáo [Portuguese Translation, 2003].
2002	*Radical Optimism: Practical Spirituality in an Uncertain World* [Second Edition with a new Preface]. Boulder, CO: Sentinent Publications.
	Radikaler Optimismus: Praktische Spiritualität in einer unsicheren Welt [German Translation, 2007].
2003	*Merton and Judaism: Recognition, Repentance, and Renewal* [Edited Volume]. Louisville, KY: Fons Vitae.
2005	*The Holy Thursday Revolution.* Maryknoll, NY: Orbis Books.

Book Collaborations

1970	"Teilhard de Chardin: The Amorization of the World," *Essays on Love, Center of Christian Experience,* eds. R. Chervin and J. Blystone.
1972	"Conscious Human Fellowship: Sri Aurobindo and Teilhard de Chardin on 'The Collective,'" *Towards Eternity,* ed. M. Reddy.
1974	"The Image of the Virgin Mother," *Women and Religion,* eds. J. Plaskow and J.A. Romero.
1975	"Science and the Psychic Grids," *Seminar on Theosophy and Science: Science and Its Impact on Society.*
1976	"The Unknown Goddess," *The Feminine Principle.*
1977	"Mother of the World to Come," *The Next Future,* ed. M. P. Pandit.

1980   "Freedom: If Anyone Is in Christ, That Person Is a New Creation," *Who Do People Say I Am?,* ed. Francis Eigo, OSA.

1984   "Da 'dominus' ad 'amicus': il ruolo della contemplazione nella transizione verso 'un nuovo ordine sociale,'" *Contemplazione e ricerca spirituale nella societa secolarizzata: La proposta di Merton a di Maritain,* eds. D.P. Patnaik and A.O. Simon.

1989   "The Unknown Goddess," *The Goddess Re-Awakening,* ed. Shirley Nicholson.

1989   "Global Spirituality," *Cross Currents,* ed. W. Birmingham.

1990   "An Ecumenical Approach to Contemplative Practice, On Being Observant, and Deep Ecology and Generic Spirituality," *Silence in the Midst of Noise,* ed. B. Bruteau.

1991   "Communitarian Non-Dualism," *As We Are One: Essays and Poems in Honor of Bede Griffiths,* ed. B. Bruteau.

1994   "The Theotokos Project," *Embracing Earth: Catholic Approaches to Ecology,* eds. A.J. LaChance and J.E. Carroll.

1996   "The One and the Many: Communitarian Non-Dualism," *The Other Half of My Soul: Bede Griffiths and the Hindu-Christian Dialogue.*

1996   "Sabbath Consciousness," *Finding a Way: Essays on Spiritual Practice,* ed. L. Zirker.

1996   "The Planetary Parliament," *The Community of Religions: Voices and Images of the Parliament of the World's Religions,* eds. Wayne Teasdale and G.F. Cairns.

1997   "Renunciation, and Forgiveness," *Woman, Why Are You Weeping,* ed. T.J. Borchard.

1997   "Eucharistic Cosmos," *The Merton Annual: Studies in Culture, Spirituality, and Social Concerns, Volume 10,* ed. V.A. Kramer.

1998   "Creator God, and God Is Present in All," *Let it Be,* ed. T.J. Borchard.

2000	"Ashram Life in the Twenty-First Century: The Integration of Polarities," *Saccidanandaya Namah: A Commemorative Volume.*
2002	"Eating Together: The Shared Supper and the Covenant Community," *Land, Community and Culture*, eds. N. Baharanyi, R. Zabawa, and W. Hill.
2003	"A Portrait of Women Spiritual Leaders in America [An Interview with Malka Drucker]," *White Fire.*
2003	"Sharing a Sacred Supper: The Moral Role of a 'Superpower,'" *Spiritual Perspectives on America's Role as Superpower.*

Articles

1971	"Sri Aurobindo and the Vision of the New Age," *Portal*, VII.
1972	"Teilhard de Chardin: The Amorization of the World," *World Union*, XI.
1972	"Sri Aurobindo and Teilhard de Chardin on the Problem of Action," *International Philosophical Quarterly*, XII.
1972	"Review of 'Evolution in Religion: A Study of Sri Aurobindo and Pierre Teilhard de Chardin,'" by R.C. Zaehner," *International Philosophical Quarterly*, XII.
1973	"The Image of the Virgin Mother," *The American Theosophist* 61.
Dec. 1973	"The Divine Mother and the Convergence of the World," *World Union* Souvenir Volume.
Dec. 1973	"Is World-Negation Taught by the Indian Scriptures?," *Mother India.*
Dec. 1974	"The Return of the Goddess," *The American Theosophist.*
Winter 1975	"The Grid-Maker," *Fields within Fields.*
Jan. 1975	"The Activation of Human Energy: Spiritual Evolution Toward Omega," *Prabuddha Bharata* [*Awakened India*], LXXX.

March 1975	"The Activation of Human Energy: Pan-Christism and the World to Come," *Prabuddha Bharata* [*Awakened India*], LXXX.
April 1975	"The Activation of Human Energy: Faith in the Future, Zest for Life," *Prabuddha Bharata* [*Awakened India*], LXXX.
Spring 1975	"The Search for the Sacred," *Human Dimensions*.
Fall 1975	"The Whole World: A Convergence Perspective," *Anima*.
April 1976	"The Unknown Goddess," *The American Theosophist*.
Oct./Nov. 1976	"A Feminine Image of God," *Mother India*.
Jan. 1977	"Mother of the World to Come," *World Union*.
Feb. 1977	"The Image of the Virgin Mother," *Mother India*.
Spring 1977	"Neo-Feminism and the Next Revolution in Consciousness," *Anima*.
Summer 1977	"Neo-Feminism and the Next Revolution in Consciousness ," *Cross Currents*, XXVII.
March 1978	"Profiles in Greatness: Pierre Teilhard de Chardin," *Prabuddha Bharata*, LXXXIII.
July 1978	"The Holy Thursday Revolution," *Liturgy*.
Fall 1978	"Neo-Feminism as Communion Consciousness," *Anima*.
March 1979	"Humanity in the Image of the Trinitarian God," *Praduddha Bharata*.
Nov. 1979	"Education for Creativity," *World Union*.
1980	"Review of *The Philosophical Approach to God: A Neo-Thomist Perspective*, by W. N. Clarke, S.J. ," *Wake Forest* [University Magazine].
Sept. 1980	"The Psychic Grid," *International Philosophical Quarterly*.
Spring 1981	"Prayer and Identity," *Contemplative Review*.
June 1981	"Education for Creativity," *The Theosophist*.
Nov. 1981	"Teilhard de Chardin and Creative Freedom," *Pra buddha Bharata*.

Fall 1981	"The Holy Thursday Revolution [Three Lectures]," *The Wilson College Quarterly.*
Fall 1981	"From Dominus to Amicus: Contemplative Insight and a New Social Order," *Cross Currents,* XXXI.
1983	"The Living One," *Cistercian Studies,* XVIII.
Jul./Aug. 1983	"Insight and Manifestation: A Way of Prayer in a Christian Context," *Prabuddha Bharata.*
Fall 1983	"Prayer and Identity, Insight and Manifestation, and The Prayer of Faith," *Contemplative Review.*
Sept./Oct. 1983	"Persons in Communion: Perichoresis," *The Theosophist.*
Jan. 1984	"Activating Human Energy," *Cistercian Studies,* XIX.
Jul./Aug. 1984	"In the Cave of the Heart: Silence and Realization," *New Blackfriars.*
1985	"Entering the Heart of Jesus," *Cistercian Studies,* XX.
1985	"Global Spirituality and the Integration of East and West," *Cross Currents,* XXXV.
1986	"Review of *On Love and Happiness,* by Pierre Teilhard de Chardin," *Cistercian Studies,* XXI.
1987	"Trinitarian Personhood," *Cistercian Studies,* XXII.
Fall 1988	"Following Jesus into Faith," *The Journal of Christian Healing* X.
Summer 1989	"The Finite and the Infinite," *The Quest* II.
1989	"Trinitarian World," *Cistercian Studies,* XXIV.
Jul./Aug	"Gospel Zen," *Living Prayer.*
Summer 1989	"The Immaculate Conception, Our Original Face," *Cross Currents,* XXXIX.
Feb. 1990	"From the Hurting Chain to the Freedom Chain," *Fellowship in Prayer.*
March/April 1990	"Practice to Become Whole," *Living Prayer.*
March 1990	"The Great Sabbath," *New Blackfriars.*

May 1990	"The Validity of Mysticism," *The Theosophist.*
Aug./Sept. 1990	"Second Sight: Looking at the World with New Eyes," *The Theosophist.*
Winter 1990–91	"Eucharistic Ecology and Ecological Spirituality," *Cross Currents*, XL.
1991	"On Being Observant," *Cistercian Studies*, XXVI.
Spring 1991	"Une Ecole du Silence," *Initiations* [Belgium].
March 1991	"Notes for an Easter Contemplation," *The Theosophist.*
June 1991	"Contemplative Life," *The Theosophist.*
Sept. 1991	"Book Review of *Merton and Walsh on the Person*, by Robert Imperato," *International Philosophical Quarterly*, XXXI.
Fall 1991	"The Word of God/Us," *Cross Currents.*
Jan. 1992	On Being Observant," *The Theosophist.*
Spring 1993	"Apprenticing to Jesus the Healer," *The Journey of Christian Healing.*
Jul./Aug. 1993	"The Trinitarian Community," *Living Prayer.*
Dec. 1993	"Esoteric Christianity ," *The Theosophist.*
Winter 1994	"Monastic Interreligious Dialogue," *Vedanta Free Press.*
Winter 1994	"Dom Bede Griffiths: Vedantic Christian," *Vedanta Free Press.*
April 1994	"An Easter Contemplation," *Fellowship in Prayer.*
Fall 1994	"Remain in Bhavamukha," *Vedanta Free Press*, 3.2.
Sept. 1994	"The Sign of Contradiction, Part I," *Living Prayer.*
Jan. 1995	"The Sign of Contradiction, Part II: 'Living Is Dying,'" *Living Prayer.*
Jan. 1995	"Take Up Your Bed and Walk," *Spirit and Life.*
March/April 1995	"Giving Is Gaining," *Living Prayer.*
Jan. 1995	"Nicodemus by Night," *Sisters Today*, 67.1.

March/April 1995	"The Sign of Contradiction, Part III: 'Giving Is Gaining,'" *Living Prayer.*
March/April 1995	"I Call You Friends," *Spirit and Life.*
Spring 1995	"The Both-And Principle," *Vedanta Free Press,* 3.3.
Summer 1995	"Householder Monastics: A New Venture," *American Vedantist.*
July/Aug. 1995	"The Seven Husbands of the Samaritan Woman," *Living Prayer.*
Nov./Dec. 1995	"Feast of St. Andrew," *Living Prayer.*
Spring 1996	"The Cosmic Context: Building the World," *American Vedantist.*
Sept./Oct. 1996	"The Emmaus Journey and the Elevation of the Holy Cross," *Spirit and Life.*
Fall 1996	"Vivekananda's Vedanta as American Vedanta," *American Vedantist.*
Nov./Dec. 1996	"What Is a Saint?," *Spirit and Life.*
Jan./Feb. 1997	"The Eucharist of Everyday Life," *Spirit and Life.*
Spring 1997	"A Vital Tradition," *American Vedantist.*
Nov./Dec. 1997	"Creation Awaits," *Spirit and Life.*
Jan. 1998	"The Path through Human Consciousness," *The Theosophist.*
May 1998	"The New Wholeness, or Life in the Planetary Village," *The Theosophist.*
Summer 1998	"Creative Spirituality: Knowing by Being," *The Quest.*
June 1998	"The New Wholeness, or Life in the Planetary Village, Part II," *The Theosophist.*
July/Aug. 1998	"The Profound Child," *Spirit and Life.*
July 1998	"The New Wholeness, or Life in the Planetary Village, Part III: Conclusion," *The Theosophist.*
Summer 1998	"Divine Action," *American Vedantist,* 4.2.
Summer 1998	"Creative Spirituality," *The Quest.*

Jan./Feb. 1999	"Jesus' Meditation," *Spirit and Life*.
March/April 1999	"Jesus, the Living Torah," *Spirit and Life*.
March 1999	"Living Is Dying," *The Theosophist*.
Aug. 1999	"The Sign of Contradiction," *The Theosophist*.
Nov./Dec. 1999	"Advent: Desiring the Infinite," *Spirit and Life*.
Nov. 1999	"Giving Is Gaining," *The Theosophist*.
Jan./Feb. 2000	"Jesus' Baptism: Back to the Beginning," *Spirit and Life*.
March/April 2000	"The Church's Banquet," *Spirit and Life*.
Spring 2000	"Theology and Practice of Social Service," *American Vedantist*.
June 2000	"The Planetary Parliament," *The Theosophist*.
Fall 2000	"Toxic Work and the Time Bind: Can Vedanta Help?," *American Vedantist*.
Winter 2001	"The Rainbow Covenant: An Ecological Spirituality," *American Vedantist*.
May/June 2001	"Virtues of Apostleship," *Spirit and Life*.
June 2001	"The Scandal of Exclusivism," *The Theosophist*.
Summer 2001	"The Witness Self," *American Vedantist*.
Jan./Feb. 2001	"Adversity and Destiny," *Spirit and Life*.
Winter 2002	"The Scandal of Exclusivity," *American Vedantist*.
Winter 2003	"Philosophy as Spiritual Practice," *American Vedantist*.
March 2003	"Mysticism, Self-Discovery, and Social Transformation," *The Quest*.
Fall 2003	"The Jesus Supper: A Full Eucharist," *The Golden String*.
2003	"Eating Together: The Shared Supper and the Covenant Community," *The Merton Annual*, XVI.
Summer 2004	"A Eucharistic Path to God-Union and Creativity," *American Vedantist*.

Summer 2005	"The Unknown Goddess," *American Vedantist*.
Fall 2005	"Theotokos and Shekhinah," *American Vedantist*.
Winter 2006	"Finding Novelty in an Old Religion," *American Vedantist*.
Sept. 2006	"Mysticism and Social Transformation," *Prabuddha Bharata*, III.
Oct. 2006	"Mysticism and Social Transformation," *Prabuddha Bharata*, III.
Nov. 2006	"Dancing Shiva and the Self-Creating World," *Prabuddha Bharata*, III.
Dec. 2006	"Dancing Shiva and the Self-Creating World," *Prabuddha Bharata*, III.
Spring 2007	"Facing Fanaticism: Vivekananda's Spiritual Democracy," *American Vedantist*, 13.1.
Summer 2007	"Vivekananda's American Vedanta," *American Vedantist*, 13.2.
Summer 2007	"Saving Jesus," *Radical Grace*, 20.3.
April/June	"The Infinite Zero," *Radical Grace* 21.2.

Interviews

Sept./Oct. 1995	"East Teaches West: An Interview with Beatrice Bruteau, by Rich Heffer," *Praying*.
April 1997	"Entering Easter: Five Spiritual Exercises for Your Journey into Deeper Life, interview by David L. Miller," *The Lutheran*.
Spring/Summer 2002	"A Song That Goes on Singing, interview by Amy Edelstein and Ellen Daly," *What Is Enlightenment?*
Spring/Summer 2006	"A Song That Goes on Singing, interview by Amy Edelstein and Ellen Daly [Reprint with introduction by Elizabeth Debold]," *What Is Enlightenment?*

Miscellaneous Pieces

1972   "God of My Life [Poem]," *New Catholic World*.

1973   *Patterns of Power in an Intercommunicating Universe* [Monograph].

1975   "God of My Life [Poem, Reprint]," *Mother of India*.

1999   Preface for *The Mystic Heart* by Wayne Teasdale, with a Forward by H.H. The Dalai Lama.

Index